WALKING ON JERSEY

About the Author

Paddy Dillon is a prolific walker and guidebook writer, with over 40 books to his name. He is an indefatigable long-distance walker who has walked all of Britain's National Trails and several major European trails. He has led guided walking holidays and has walked throughout Europe, as well as in Nepal, Tibet and the Rocky Mountains of Canada and the US.

Paddy has walked extensively around all the Channel Islands, delighting in island-hopping. While exploring Jersey he has walked around the coast several times, enjoying urban promenades, sandy beach walks, clifftop paths, rugged headlands and secluded coves. He has also penetrated far inland, into deep wooded valleys, along quiet traffic-calmed 'green lanes', passing potato fields and pastures grazed by contented Jersey cows.

Other Cicerone guides by the author:

GR20: Corsica
Irish Coastal Walks
The Cleveland Way and the
   Yorkshire Wolds Way
The GR5 Trail
The Great Glen Way
The Irish Coast to Coast Walk
The Mountains of Ireland
The National Trails
The North York Moors
The Pennine Way
The Reivers Way
The South West Coast Path
The Teesdale Way

Trekking in Greenland
Trekking through Mallorca
Walking in County Durham
Walking in Madeira
Walking in Mallorca
Walking in Malta
Walking in the Isles of Scilly
Walking in the North Pennines
Walking on Guernsey
Walking on the Isle of Arran
Walking on La Gomera and
   El Hierro
Walking on La Palma
Walking the Galloway Hills

WALKING ON JERSEY

by

Paddy Dillon

2 POLICE SQUARE, MILNTHORPE, CUMBRIA LA7 7PY
www.cicerone.co.uk

© Paddy Dillon 2011
First edition 2011
ISBN: 978 1 85284 638 1

This book is one of two new guides to walking on the Channel Islands, replacing Paddy Dillon's previous Cicerone guide:
Channel Island Walks
ISBN-10: 1 85284 288 1
ISBN-13: 978 1 85284 288 8

Printed by KHL Printing, Singapore.
A catalogue record for this book is available from the British Library.
All photographs are by the author.

Advice to Readers

Readers are advised that, while every effort is made by our authors to ensure the accuracy of guidebooks as they go to print, changes can occur during the lifetime of an edition. Please check Updates on this book's page on the Cicerone website (www.cicerone.co.uk) before planning your trip. We would also advise that you check information about such things as transport, accommodation and shops locally. Even rights of way can be altered over time. We are always grateful for information about any discrepancies between a guidebook and the facts on the ground, sent by email to info@ cicerone.co.uk or by post to Cicerone, 2 Police Square, Milnthorpe LA7 7PY, United Kingdom.

Front cover: Mont Orgueil Castle above Gorey Harbour

CONTENTS

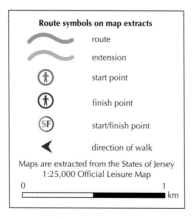

Route symbols on map extracts

route

extension

start point

finish point

start/finish point

direction of walk

Maps are extracted from the States of Jersey
1:25,000 Official Leisure Map

Location of walks

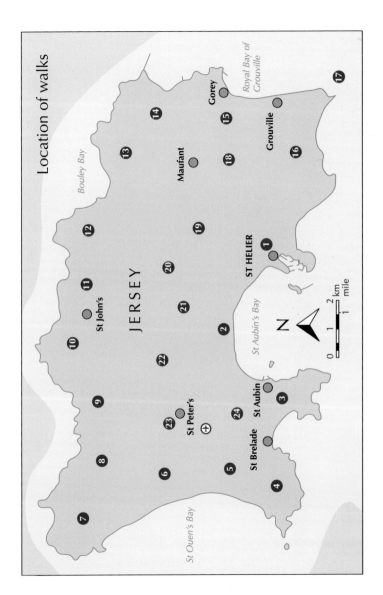

Le Sentier des Moulins follows a path running alongside an old mill race in Waterworks Valley (Walk 21)

INTRODUCTION

*'Morceaux de France tombés à la mer
et ramassés par l'Angleterre.'*
*'Pieces of France fallen into the sea
and picked up by England.'*

Victor Hugo

Small and often very busy, but also beautiful and abounding in interest, the Channel Islands are an intriguing walking destination. The self-governing 'Bailiwicks' of Jersey and Guernsey owe their allegiance to the Crown and seem outwardly British, but are in fact an ancient remnant of the Duchy of Normandy, with Norman–French place-names very much in evidence. For British visitors it is like being at home and abroad at the same time. French visitors, however, find it a quintessentially British experience!

Walkers will find magnificent cliff and coastal paths, golden sandy beaches, wooded valleys and quiet country lanes. Flowers will be noticed everywhere and there is a rich birdlife. There are castles, churches, ancient monuments and fortifications to visit, as well as a host of other attractions. There are efficient and frequent bus services, and easy onward links by air and sea between the islands. This guidebook describes 24 one-day walking routes on Jersey, covering a total distance around 225km (140 miles), plus a long-distance coastal walk around the island, measuring almost 80km (50 miles). There is also a note about the Channel Islands Way, a long-distance island-hopping route embracing the entire archipelago, covering 178km (110 miles).

LOCATION

The Channel Islands lie south of Britain, but not everyone immediately appreciates how close they are to France. The islands fit snugly into a box bounded by lines of longitude 2°W and 3°W, and lines of latitude 49°N and 50°N. This puts them well and truly in the Golfe de St Malo off the Normandy coast of France, The French refer to them as *Les Îles Anglo-Normandes*, and that is the clue to their curious place in geography and history. They are the only remnants of the Duchy of Normandy to remain loyal to the Crown.

Jersey is the largest and southern-most of the islands, yet has an area of only 116km² (45 square miles). No point on the island is more than 3.5km (2 miles) from the sea, yet it can take weeks to explore the place thoroughly.

9

GEOLOGY

In Britain virtually every major geological period is represented. Channel Islands geology is more closely related to structures in France. Rocks are either very ancient or relatively recent, with hundreds of millions of years missing from the middle of the geological timescale. Fossils are virtually absent and the amount of sedimentary rock is quite limited. Most of the area is made up of ancient sediments and igneous rocks which have been heated, warped, crushed, deformed, melted and metamorphosed. Further intrusions of igneous rocks cause further confusion for the beginner, but there is a basic succession that can be presented in a simplified form.

The most ancient bedrocks in the Channel Islands are metamorphic and metasediment rocks known as 'Pentevrian' – a term used in neighbouring France. Ancient gneisses, often containing xenoliths of other long-lost strata, feature in this early series. Dating rocks of this type is possible only by measuring radio-isotopes in their mineral structures, which suggest dates of formation ranging from 2500 to 1000 million years ago. The oldest rocks occur in southern Guernsey, western Alderney and possibly on Sark.

The 'Brioverian' sedimentary series dates from 900 to 700 million years ago. It is represented by a broad band of mudstones, siltstones and conglomerates through Jersey.

10

In Guernsey only a small area in the west contains these rocks, though in an altered state. One of the problems of dealing with these sediments is that even while they were being formed, they were being deformed by earthquakes, heat and pressure. Fossil remains are few, and in fact are represented only by a few worm burrows.

Following on from the formation of the Brioverian sediments, a series of igneous intrusions were squeezed into the rocks around 650 to 500 million years ago. Interestingly, both granites and gabbros were intruded, along with intermediate rock types. A host of minor sills, dykes and pipes were injected to further complicate matters. These tough, speckled, igneous rocks have been quarried all over the Channel Islands for local building and for export.

Events during the next 500 million years are conjectural, and based on geological happenings elsewhere in Britain and France. Rocks from this span of time are absent, though they are known from the surrounding sea bed. On dry land, sediments date only from the past couple of million years; as this was a time of ice ages, indications are that the climate varied from sub-tropical to sub-arctic. Sea levels fluctuated so that both raised beaches and sunken forests and peat bogs can be discerned. For much of the time, the Channel Islands were part of one landmass with Britain and France, but rising sea levels formed the English Channel and, one by one, each of the

Jersey's geology can be studied while walking around its rugged cliff coastline

Channel Islands. Guernsey became an island around 14,000 years ago while Jersey became an island around 7000 years ago.

Exhibits relating to the geology of Jersey can be studied at the Jersey Museum and La Hougue Bie. The British Geological Survey publishes detailed geological maps of the Channel Islands and there are a number of publications dealing with the subject.

TURBULENT HISTORY

Little is known of the customs and traditions of nomadic Palaeolithic Man, but he hunted mammoth and woolly rhinoceros when Jersey was still part of the European mainland 200,000 years ago. Neolithic and Bronze Age people made many magnificent monuments which are dotted around the Channel Islands. Henges, mounds, tombs, and mysterious menhirs were raised by peoples whose origins are unclear and whose language is unknown. What is certain is that they had a reverence for their dead and were obviously living in well-ordered communities able to turn their hands to the construction of such mighty structures. The Romans knew of these islands, though whether they wholly colonised them or simply had an occupying presence and trading links is a matter of debate.

St Helier lived on a rocky islet, protecting Jersey by the power of prayer, until beheaded by pirates in the year 555. The basic parish structure of the Channel Islands, and most of the parish churches, date from around this period. No doubt the position of the Channel Islands made them a favourite spot for plundering by all and sundry on the open sea. The Norsemen were regular raiders in the 9th century, and by the 10th century they were well established in the territory of Normandy. It was from

The Channel Islands Occupation Society preserves some military sites as visitor attractions

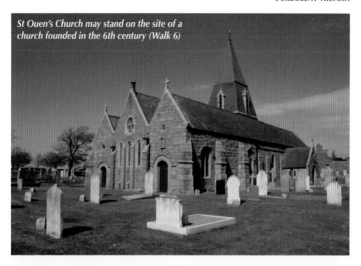

St Ouen's Church may stand on the site of a church founded in the 6th century (Walk 6)

Normandy that Duke William I, 'The Longsword', claimed the islands as his own in the year 933, and they have been part of the Duchy of Normandy ever since.

Duke William II, 'The Conqueror', defeated Harold at the Battle of Hastings in 1066. When King John lost Normandy to France in 1204, the Channel Islands remained loyal and were granted special privileges and a measure of self-government that continues to this day. However, the islands were repeatedly attacked, invaded and partially occupied by French forces throughout the Hundred Years War. During the most turbulent times of strife, the Pope himself intervened and decreed in 1483 that the Channel Islands should be neutral in those conflicts. The islanders were able to

turn the situation to their advantage, trading with both sides! Church control passed from the French Diocese of Coutances to the English Diocese of Winchester in 1568.

During the English Civil War in the 17th century, the islands were divided against themselves, with Jersey for the Crown and Guernsey for Parliament. The French invaded the islands for the last time in 1781; stout defensive structures were raised against any further threats, particularly during the Napoleonic Wars, and in fact well into the 19th century. Queen Victoria visited the Channel Islands three times to inspect military developments.

During the First World War the Channel Islands escaped virtually unscathed, though the local

13

Gerry built! One of several prominent concrete structures built during the German Occupation

militia forces were disbanded, and many of those who joined the regular army were slaughtered elsewhere in Europe. In the Second World War, after the fall of France to the German army, the Channel Islands were declared indefensible and were demilitarised. Many islanders evacuated to England, particularly from Alderney, but others stayed behind and suffered for five years under the German Occupation. Massive fortifications made the Channel Islands the most heavily defended part of Hitler's Atlantic Wall.

There were only token raids and reconnaissances by British forces, and the Channel Islands were completely by-passed during the D-Day landings in nearby Normandy. VE Day in Europe was 8th May 1945, but the Channel Islands weren't liberated until 9th May, as it was unclear whether the German garrison would surrender without a fight. The Channel Islands Occupation Society, www. ciosjersey.org.uk, publishes a number of books and journals about the war years, including an annual review. Various military structures from the Occupation have been preserved as visitor attractions.

The modern development of the Channel Islands has been in two directions. As a holiday destination it caters for a multitude of tastes, with an emphasis on sun, sea, fun, family, good food and the outdoors. In the financial services sector the low rate of taxation has brought in billions of pounds of investment and attracted a population of millionaires. The Channel Islands retain some quirky laws and customs, enjoy a low crime rate, issue their own currency and postage stamps and enjoy a unique history and heritage that is well interpreted at a number of interesting visitor sites.

The best place to start enquiring into history is the Jersey Museum, The Weighbridge, St Helier, JE2 3NG, tel. 01534 633300. This is also the place to enquire about La Société Jersiaise, tel. 01534 758314, www.societe-jersiaise.org, and Jersey Heritage, www.jerseyheritage.org. The 'Jersey Pass' can be purchased, allowing entry to all the sites managed by Jersey Heritage. There are numerous publications available examining all aspects of Channel Islands history. Detail is often intense, and any historical building or site mentioned in this guidebook probably has one or more books dedicated entirely to it.

Another organisation involved with heritage matters is the National Trust for Jersey, The Elms, La Chève Rue, St Mary, JE3 3EN, tel. 01534 483193, www.nationaltrustjersey.org.je. The Trust owns land and properties around Jersey, several of which are visited on walks throughout this guidebook. At the last count the trust owned 16 properties, cared for a number of others, and owned 1.6% of the land in Jersey, making it the biggest landowner after the States of Jersey. The National Trust for Jersey has reciprocal agreements with the National Trust of Guernsey, National Trust of England, Wales and Northern Ireland, and National Trust for Scotland, allowing members free entry to properties that normally levy a charge.

GOVERNMENT

The Channel Islands are a quirky little archipelago, with startling divisions among themselves. They are neither colonies nor dependencies. They are not part of the United Kingdom or the European Union. They have been described as 'Peculiars of the Crown' meaning that they are practically the property of the Crown, and they owe their allegiance to the Crown, and not to Parliament.

There are actually two self-governing Bailiwicks whose law-making processes are quite separate from those of the United Kingdom's Parliament. Furthermore, the Bailiwick of Jersey's affairs are quite separate from the Bailiwick of Guernsey. A thorough investigation of Channel Islands government is an absorbing study, which anyone with political inclinations might like to investigate while walking around the islands. Check the States of Jersey government website for further information, www.gov.je, as well as the States Assembly website, www.statesassembly.gov.je, and the Jersey Legal Information Board, www.jerseylaw.je. Legal documents are traditionally prepared in 'Jersey Legal French', but since the year 2000 there has been a drive to make these accessible to the public by presenting them in English.

WILDLIFE

Plants

The Channel Islands are noted for their flowers, and it is possible to find wild flowers in bloom at any time of the year. The southerly, maritime disposition of the islands and their range of habitats, from fertile soil to barren rocks, ensure that a wide variety of species can thrive. Even attempting to shortlist them is a pointless exercise.

Jersey is not part of the United Kingdom, but owes its allegiance to the British Crown

Spring and early summer are the best times to visit Jersey to see wild flowers at their most colourful

The sand dunes of Les Quennevais support around 400 species, and even an old cemetery in the heart of St Helier is graced with 100 species. Bear in mind that the sea is also a bountiful source of marine plants. Add to this the plants that are cultivated in greenhouses and gardens: there are 60 varieties of roses in the Howard Davies Park, and orchids from around the world bloom at the Eric Young Orchid Centre. The study of Jersey's floral tributes becomes a vast undertaking!

Even walkers who have no great interest in flowers cannot fail to be amazed at the sight of narcissi and bluebells growing on the northern cliffs of Jersey. Add abundant swathes of sea campion, red campion, blazes of gorse and broom, nodding ox-eye daisies, and the result is a riot of colour. The sight of fleshy-leaved mesembryanthemum colonising entire cliffs is impressive and unusual. A comprehensive field guide to wild flowers is an essential companion on any walk, but make sure that it encompasses not only a good range of British plants, but also plants from the Mediterranean, which are at their northernmost limits around Jersey. La Société Jersiaise, www.societe-jersiaise.org, gathers plenty of information about Jersey's botany.

Animals

Mammoth, woolly rhinoceros and deer are known to have flourished in the past on the Channel Islands, but today Jersey is devoid of large wild mammals. Rabbits do well almost

17

everywhere, but little else is likely to be seen except for evidence of moles and small rodents. Red squirrels were introduced to Jersey by local naturalists in 1885. The Durrell Wildlife Conservation Trust features a splendid range of exotic species, but look to the sea for other species, such as dolphins. Local differences occur between the islands, such as the fact that toads are found on Jersey, but not Guernsey, though green lizards live on both islands. Insect life is abundant and varied, with a range of colourful butterflies.

The birdlife is amazingly rich, with a range of residents and a host of migratory species. While the landmass is rather small to support many raptors, there are owls, kestrels and sparrowhawks. The coastal margins abound in interest, attracting a range of waders which probe the beaches and rock pools for food. The cliffs and pebbly beaches provide safe nesting places for a variety of gulls and terns, and puffins can be seen on some of the smaller islands and stacks. There are areas of heathland where the rare Dartford warbler might be seen or heard, and there are a few areas of dense woodland, marsh and grassland sites which attract particular species. The range of bird habitats is under pressure from human development and recreation on such tiny islands but, even so, there is plenty to see.

Listing a couple of hundred species of birds is a pointless exercise, and so much depends on the time

A gull perches nonchalantly on a German gun at the Batterie Möltke at Les Landes

of year and prevailing conditions. A good field guide to birds is useful, and there are titles specific to the Channel Islands. The Jersey Museum has exhibits relating to natural history, and visitor centres such as the Kempt Tower offer specific information about the plants and animals. La Société Jersiaise, www.societe-jersiaise. org, produces the annual Jersey Bird Report, or see www.jerseybirds.co.uk for information.

PROTECTED AREAS

There is no national park on Jersey, though for many years the species-rich sand dunes of Les Blanches Banques near Les Quennevais have been regarded as a 'special' area, even referred to as a 'trainee national park'. There are several small nature reserves on Jersey, from marshland to woodland. The National Trust for Jersey has already been mentioned, owning 1.6% of the land area of Jersey, which they are dedicated to preserving. There are also large and very important marine reserves, some of which are particularly difficult to access. They include the southeast coast and the rocky reefs of Les Ecrehous, Les Minquiers, Les Pierres de Lecq and Les Dirouilles.

GETTING TO JERSEY

A map of transport routes makes Jersey look like the centre of the universe, with ferries and flights converging on

the island from all points of the compass. Bear in mind that there are seasonal variations, with more services available in the summer months than in the winter.

WHO CAN GO?

People who hold British or European Union passports or identity cards do not need visas to visit Jersey. All air travellers must produce some form of photo-ID or they may be denied boarding. People who have obtained a visa to visit Britain can also visit Jersey during the period for which their visa is valid. Dogs and other pets can be brought from Britain to Jersey, subject to any conditions that might be imposed by ferry or flight operators. Usual practice applies to walking dogs in the countryside; keep them under control, especially near livestock. Dogs may be barred from beaches during the summer months and anti-fouling laws are in place everywhere.

FLIGHTS

Direct flights to Jersey operate from more than two dozen British airports, along with a few direct flights from countries such as Ireland, France and Germany. Both scheduled and charter flights are available. Scheduled flights are mostly operated by Flybe, www.flybe.com, Bmibaby, www.bmibaby.com and Blue Islands, www.blueislands.com, with Aurigny,

The National Trust for Jersey is a major landowner, maintaining some interesting short walks

www.aurigny.com and Blue Islands operating most of the inter-island flights. Summer charter flights are mainly operated by Channel Islands Travel Group, www.jerseytravel.com. This is not an exhaustive list and choices are quite bewildering, so it takes time to sift and sort between the operators, schedules and prices, but with patience some extraordinarily good deals can be found.

FERRIES

Ferries serve Jersey from Britain and France. Ferries from Britain are operated by Condor, www.condorferries.co.uk, sailing from Weymouth, Poole and Portsmouth. Passengers can choose between fast and slow ships, either travelling directly to Jersey

or via a short break at Guernsey. Condor also serves Jersey from St Malo in France. Other ferry services from France are operated by Manche Îles Express, www.manche-iles-express.com, sailing from Granville and Barnville-Carteret to Jersey, also offering links with Guernsey, Alderney and Sark.

TOUR OPERATORS

Package holidays to the Channel Islands can be arranged for any period from a weekend upwards, freeing you from the hassle of trying to co-ordinate ferries, flights, accommodation and meals. Prices are quite competitive and there are seasonal variations, so it pays to shop around for the best deals.

WHEN TO GO

Jersey is suitable as a year-round destination and generally enjoys slightly milder weather than the south of England, but the weather is still highly variable and impossible to forecast accurately. Winters are mild, but there may be frosts and, very occasionally, snow. Very bad weather at any time of year can upset ferry schedules, while fog affects flights. The peak summer period can be very hot and busy, which may not suit those looking for peace and quiet. The shoulder seasons, spring and autumn, are generally ideal for walking, with bright, clear days and temperatures that are neither too high nor too low. In fact, these are the times of year that the Jersey Walking Weeks are arranged, featuring plenty of guided walks led by local experts.

ACCOMMODATION

Jersey offers every type of accommodation to suit every pocket, but over the past few years prices have risen as hotels have moved up-market. Choose an accommodation base carefully, thinking primarily about how you intend to organise your walks. If you are hiring a car, then any base anywhere on the island will be fine. If you intend using the bus services to travel to and from walks, then the best

Visiting walkers can join local walkers during the spring and autumn Walking Weeks

21

base would be somewhere central in St Helier, handy for the bus station. An annual accommodation guide is produced, which can be obtained by post from Jersey Tourism, or browsed online at www.jersey.com.

Visitors who want to hire unusual historic properties should look at some of the holiday lets available through Jersey Heritage and the National Trust for Jersey. A number of interesting old military properties have been converted into self-catering accommodation for families and groups; however, they are not advertised widely and do not feature in the usual holiday brochures.

HEALTH AND SAFETY

There are no nasty diseases on Jersey, or at least, nothing you couldn't contract at home. Domestic water supplies are fed from either reservoirs or underground sources, sometimes augmented by a desalination plant. Treated water is perfectly drinkable, but some people don't like the taste and prefer to buy bottled water, which is quite expensive. There are no snakes and no stinging insects worse than wasps and bees.

In case of a medical emergency, dial 999 (or the European emergency number 112) for an ambulance. In case of a non-emergency, there are chemists, doctors, dentists and a hospital. At the time of writing (and this may change from 2011) there is no reciprocal health agreement between Jersey and the United Kingdom, nor is there any point in carrying the European Health Insurance Card. If emergency treatment is required it will be provided, but in order to avoid a large bill it may be necessary to carry appropriate insurance.

FOOD AND DRINK

Jersey has long prided itself on being intensively agricultural, though this is waning and farmers face an uncertain future. In the past, the island was famous for its cider-apple orchards, but these were largely cleared as farmers began to experiment with potato-growing. The name 'Jersey' immediately conjures images of delicious 'Jersey Royal' potatoes, which were originally known as 'Jersey Royal Fluke'. This variety was developed from two potatoes that were given to Hugh de la Haye in the early 1800s. The potato even has its own website, www.jerseyroyals.co.uk.

The name 'Jersey' also conjures images of contented brown cows giving rich, creamy milk for butter and ice-cream. Jersey cows have a long pedigree and have always been immensely important on the island. Laws were passed in the 18th and 19th centuries to restrict the importation of cattle, so that the unique qualities of Jersey cows were protected. Jersey herds are admired and renowned world-wide, and they too have their own website, www.jersey dairy.je.

Jersey Royals, best eaten freshly-picked while on Jersey, with a knob of Jersey butter

Some Jersey foodstuffs are enjoying a revival, most notably 'Black Butter', which is neither black nor butter, but a concoction of cider-apples, liquorice and spices, with an intriguing flavour that goes well with sweet or savoury foodstuffs. A German tourist observed, 'It tastes like Christmas!' Black Butter is produced by La Mare Wine Estate along with wines, spirits and a range of quality mustards, preserves, biscuits and chocolates, www. lamarewineestate.com.

Naturally, Jersey offers good seafood, but one of the greatest delicacies is unlikely to be savoured by visitors. The 'ormer', or abalone, is a marine mollusc that can only be gathered at certain times and there are plenty of restrictions in place to conserve the species. As a result it tends to be eaten primarily by Jersey folk, with nothing left over for commercial restaurants.

Of course, Jersey also imports plenty of food and drink, both British and international goods, from simple, low-priced products to expensive quality items. On the whole, expect things to cost a little more than in Britain, and bear in mind that most supermarkets and shops are in St Helier, and not every village has a shop. On the other hand, pubs, restaurants, cafés and snack kiosks are regularly encountered while walking round Jersey, and places offering refreshments are mentioned in the route descriptions. Food offered ranges from basic snacks to *haute cuisine*, and as it is easy to get from place to place for food and drink, you need

23

Granite cliffs and wooded slopes below La Grosse Tête are best seen from the sea (Walk 4)

only be guided by your palate and spending limits.

PARLEZ-VOUS FRANGLAIS?

For centuries the language commonly spoken around the Channel Islands was a Norman– French 'patois' which had distinct forms from island to island. The Jersey form is known as *Jèrriais*, and while it is rarely heard, it is still spoken and many people are keen to preserve it. Sometimes it is referred to as 'Jersey French', but a French person would struggle to understand it. It also goes by the name of 'Jersey Norman French' and 'Jersey Norman'. It should not be confused with 'Jersey Legal French', which is mostly modern French, with a few archaic Jersey words, used for drafting legal documents.

Visiting walkers may hear nothing of the language, but will be very aware of the roots of the language

preserved in place-names all over the island. Some modern signs are bilingual, in English and Jèrriais. The latest banknotes produced by the States of Jersey are trilingual – English, Jèrriais and French – so that 'one pound' is also rendered as *un louis* and *une livre*. Visitors with a good knowledge of French will probably pronounce the place-names with a French accent, but in fact the 'correct' pronunciation would be different. In all other respects, English is spoken, written and understood everywhere, but there are also sizeable Portuguese (mostly Madeiran) and Polish communities on the island, as well as resident and visiting nationals from many other countries. It is increasingly common to hear French, German, Dutch and Japanese spoken on the streets. If assistance is needed with the pronunciation of a place-name, the best person to ask is a Jersey person!

MONEY

The States of Jersey issue their own banknotes and coins, which are inextricably linked to Sterling and come in exactly the same denominations. However, Jersey one and two pound coins are rare, while Jersey one pound notes are common. Bank of England Sterling notes and coins can be spent in Jersey, and currency issued by the States of Guernsey is also accepted. In theory, Sterling banknotes from Scotland and Northern Ireland are accepted, but this depends on whether the person to whom you are offering them is familiar with them. Some businesses will accept Euros, but the rate of exchange may be poor. Change given at the close of a transaction may be a mixture of Jersey and British currency. Remember that Jersey currency is not legal tender in Britain, though British banks will change notes at face value. It is common for visitors approaching the end of a holiday in Jersey to request British currency only in their change. Your last few Jersey coins can be dropped in a charity box on departure, or saved as mementos of your visit.

Jersey specialises in financial services and banks from all over the world are represented on the streets of St Helier. ATMs are common and a wide variety of credit and debit cards are accepted by businesses. There is no VAT on purchases and the island enjoys a low rate of tax. There is an advantage in purchasing some high-value items on the island, but the cost of transporting goods to Jersey can make some of the benefits marginal.

COMMUNICATIONS

If taking a mobile phone to Jersey, check in advance with your service provider, or you might find yourself paying a high price for calls. The local providers are Jersey Telecom, www.jerseytelecom.com, and Sure Cable & Wireless, www.surecw.com. There is generally good mobile coverage around the island. There are telephone kiosks in most urban and some rural areas, which invariably take coins, though emergency calls (999 or 112) are free. Free Wi-Fi is available at the bus station in St Helier and some accommodation providers also offer this as a service to their guests.

Royal Mail postage stamps from Britain are not valid in Jersey. Any attempt to use them will result in delayed delivery and an excess charge for the recipient. Jersey Post stamps must be used, and if you are posting to Britain, Europe, or any other destination, make this clear when you buy stamps as there are different rates. There are half-a-dozen post offices around St Helier and most villages on the island have a post office, as well as the airport. Walkers with an interest in philately can make arrangements to collect Jersey stamps and first-day covers on a regular basis. Enquire at the Philatelic Bureau for details, www.jerseypost.com.

Jersey's north coast features a fine footpath, seen here above Bouley Bay (Walk 13)

WALKING ON JERSEY

Walking on Jersey is incredibly varied, but most people concentrate on the island's coastline

The walks in this guidebook are mostly short and straightforward, chosen to reflect the diversity of the landscapes and seascapes, along with the history, heritage and natural history of Jersey. Almost all the walks link directly with one or two other walks, allowing all kinds of extensions to the routes. All the walks are easily accessible by bus services, so a car is not necessary.

Jersey has an area of only 116km² (45 square miles) and walkers are never more than 3.5km (2 miles) from the sea. Within this limited area this guidebook offers around 225km (140 miles) of incredibly varied walking, with a coastal walk alone measuring almost 80km (50 miles). If explorations are extended to Guernsey, Alderney, Sark and Herm, then the interest and enjoyment is doubled. Complete coastal walks around the five main Channel Islands are now

being promoted as the 'Channel Islands Way', measuring 178km (110 miles).

In the past the Channel Islands were not really viewed as a walking destination; rather, they were a holiday destination where people simply couldn't help walking. These days, one third of visitors state that their main reason for visiting the islands is to walk. The sight of golden beaches, rugged cliffs, flowery headlands and lush woodlands proves irresistible for exploring on foot. There are so many things to see along the paths, tracks and roads – interesting places to visit and always the offer of food and drink.

The walks are mostly circular and almost every stretch along the coast features a contrasting exploration inland. It has to be said that there are few paths and tracks inland, and while some roads can be quite busy, there are plenty of quiet country roads

A designated 'green lane' gives priority to walkers and cyclists, with a 15mph speed limit for vehicles

Paths on Jersey are mostly on firm, dry surfaces, but some stretches may be muddy after rain. Some paths on steep slopes are equipped with plenty of wooden steps, and most of these have been made slip-proof. Most of the time, a pair of comfortable walking shoes are fine for walking, and hefty boots are not required. If boots are worn, lightweight ones will suffice. There are some signposts, but most paths are obvious even without markers, and it is usually made clear if a path is private. Roads on Jersey usually bear their names at one end or both, which saves confusion when they form a dense network.

too, specially designated as 'green lanes', where priority is given to walkers, cyclists and horse-riders. A few of the walks are entirely inland, because it is important to appreciate the inland countryside and its farming traditions just as much as the popular coastline. Almost every route passes some sort of attraction, ranging from castles to historic houses, churches to craft centres. Many attractions seem to exist purely because they have a captive audience of visitors, and those that are on or near the walks are noted, with brief details given. Many of them have an entry charge and may be well worth an hour's exploration.

WHAT TO TAKE

Generally speaking, Jersey's weather is a little milder than the weather you would expect in the south of England. There are no hills and walkers rarely find themselves much above 100m (330ft) above sea level. The most basic walking gear will suffice, with comfortable footwear and clothing to suit hot and cool conditions, including sun protection for sunny days and waterproofs in case of rain. It is increasingly common to see heavily-booted walkers with poles and packs trudging round the island, but Jersey is a gentle landscape, and even if foul weather were to interfere with a walk, it is very easy to cut walks short, bail out by bus and retreat to your lodgings.

WAYMARKING AND ACCESS

Jersey is intensively cultivated, with large areas of tillage given over to potatoes and other crops, while pastures are grazed by Jersey cows. Almost 90,000 people live on the island, the road network is remarkably dense and car ownership is very high. Add to this the huge number of visitors, and it is a wonder there is room to breathe, let alone walk. However, there are plenty of paths, tracks and quiet roads available for walkers, and while signposts and waymarks are few, routes that are freely available to the public are usually quite obvious. The best maps of Jersey show many of these routes, but by no means all of them. In practical terms, with this guidebook to hand, Jersey can be explored thoroughly using the available access.

Special mention needs to be made of the inter-tidal zone. Jersey has one of the biggest tidal ranges in the world, up to 12m (40ft) at spring tides. The sight of sandy beaches and jagged rocks emerging from the sea as the tide recedes encourages many people to explore to the water's edge, especially in the south-east. To a certain extent this is to be encouraged, but it must be done with caution. Obtain a copy of the tide tables and study them carefully. Walking out as the tide recedes is unlikely to be a problem, but when the tide is advancing it is possible to be cut off before realising it. Trying to get from beach to beach around the foot of cliffs can be dangerous and can lead to an inconvenient stranding, or death by drowning. In short, don't wander around the inter-tidal zone

A newly-planted wooden signpost, keeping visitors on course to enjoy their walks

without having a clearly visible route back to dry land.

MAPS

The maps in this guide are extracted from the States of Jersey 1:25,000 Official Leisure Map of Jersey which, in terms of style and content, is similar to the Ordnance Survey 1:25,000 Explorer maps of Britain. In fact, the map was originally compiled by the Ordnance Survey, but has since been digitised and updated by Digimap, www.digimap.je, for the States of Jersey. It is the most detailed map of the island, showing everything down to field boundaries and even the back gardens of houses in towns and villages. The walking routes in this guidebook are shown as a highlighted overlay on this map.

There are plenty of other maps of Jersey, including free maps suitable for general touring, which often highlight attractions so boldly that they obscure other details in the vicinity. By all means amass a collection of free maps, picking them up from Jersey Tourism or from hotels and visitor attractions around the island.

GETTING AROUND JERSEY

By car

Cars can be taken on the Condor ferries to Jersey, and it is possible to hire cars on Jersey, either pre-booked or

An extreme form of transport, a DUKW trundles off the beach and into the sea

on arrival. Jersey cars carry a 'J' before the number on their registration plates, but hire cars are also stamped with a prominent 'H' for 'hire' or, according to local drivers, 'horror', because of the way they perceive the driving skills of visitors! Jersey's roads are narrow and the maximum speed limit is 40mph, dropping to 15mph on 'green lanes'. Roads can be very congested, especially at peak times around St Helier, and parking is very limited in some areas. The bottom line is, you won't be going anywhere fast!

A car is essential if you choose accommodation away from a regular bus route, but if you are based in St Helier, or on a regular bus route, then it is best to use buses to travel round the island. Drivers should obtain and study the free leaflet 'Parking and Driving in Jersey'. If you do not understand the 'filter in turn' rule that applies in Jersey, then think twice before driving there.

By bus

Jersey has an excellent bus network provided by Connex, and it is worth visiting the bus station, Liberation Station, to pick up timetables and enquire about tickets at the earliest opportunity. All the routes in this guidebook were researched using buses, and this mode of travel is heartily recommended. The 'myBus' timetable comes in summer and winter versions, with only minor differences between them. In the summer months there is also an 'Explorer' timetable.

Summer visitors should of course obtain both.

The year-round 'myBus' routes are numbered and generally fan outwards from St Helier, running early until late. They reach various far-flung parts of Jersey, where they turn round and come back to town. Only a few bus routes cross each other. Tickets can be bought on the bus for single journeys and there are two prices, depending on whether the journey is short or long. Bus passes can be bought from the station, offering unlimited travel for periods ranging from one to five days, and offering progressively better value if bought for several days. In general, you need to make at least three long bus journeys per day for these passes to pay for themselves, otherwise single tickets work out cheaper.

During the summer months there are also 'Explorer' buses, which are named after colours rather than numbers. So, 'Red Explorer' does not mean that the bus will be painted red, just that it will bear that name. The 'Explorer' buses are aimed at visitors, so they do not run early or late, and their routes are structured to serve as many visitor attractions as possible. Unlike the 'myBus' routes, 'Explorer' routes often cross each other and the 'Yellow Explorer' in particular links several bus services in the north of Jersey.

Bus passes are valid on both 'myBus' and 'Explorer' services, and Connex is keen to assist walkers by producing free walking route leaflets. For full details of all bus services on Jersey, tel. 01534 877772, www.mybus.je.

TOURIST INFORMATION

The first point of contact for all tourism-related enquiries is Jersey Tourism, Liberation Place, St Helier, JE1 1BB. Tel. 01534 448800, email info@jersey.com, website www.jersey.com.

Jersey Tourism provides plenty of free printed materials, including accommodation brochures and leaflets about attractions and events and 'what's on' guides. There are also books, maps and gifts on sale. Its website includes plenty of information about walking opportunities, including the popular Jersey Walking Weeks

that are a feature of spring and autumn each year. These events offer visiting walkers the chance to explore the island in the company of Jersey people, led by knowledgeable local guides.

EMERGENCIES

The police, ambulance, fire and coastguard services are all alerted by dialling 999, free of charge, from any telephone. Alternatively, the European emergency number of 112 can be used. Jersey has two police forces, having retained an 'honorary' police force dating from the 15th century, whose officers are attached to the island parishes, www.jerseyhonorarypolice.org.

The emergency services sometimes call for the assistance of the Channel Islands Air Search, a voluntary

The black and white Noirmont Tower off Noirmont Point dates from around 1810 (Walk 3)

organisation that maintains a light aircraft, available on stand-by 24 hours a day, 365 days a year, offering an 'eyes in the sky' capability around the islands. See www.ci-airsearch.com.

USING THIS GUIDE

The walks in this guidebook start with a town trail around St Helier, allowing visitors to become acquainted with some of the heritage features and services of the largest town in the Channel Islands. Walks 2 to 16 are arranged clockwise round the coast of Jersey, and most of them are circular, made up of a coastal stretch and an inland stretch. They are all fairly short and easy, with the most rugged being along the north coast. As all the walks are arranged side-by-side they can be linked to form longer walks. Walk 17 is different, and is entirely dependent on a favourable tide; therefore it might not be possible to attempt while you are on the island. Walks 18 to 24 explore the inland parts of Jersey, though as has already been observed, no part of the island is more than 3.5km (2 miles) from the sea.

All the walking routes are accessible by bus services, and if any other bus services cross them, these are mentioned. Places offering food and drink are mentioned, but as opening times vary it is wise to carry something to eat and drink. If there are any visitor attractions on the routes, these are given a brief description, and if contact details are provided, opening times can be checked. Bear in mind that some attractions take an hour or two to explore properly, and this eats into the time spent walking. A very short walking route with two or three major attractions and a good restaurant can take all day to complete if walkers really want to make the most of these opportunities!

Some walkers visit Jersey simply to walk all the way round the coast, and this is an admirable plan. Walk 25 explains in very brief detail how to do it, by referring readers back to Walks 2 to 16. Each of these walks includes a stretch of coast, but at the point where these routes head inland, it is possible to link directly with the next walk in the book and the next stretch of coast. An annual sponsored walk aims to cover the coast in one long day, while average walkers would take three or four days to walk round the island. During the Jersey Walking Weeks, a guided five-day circuit is offered.

Walkers who have also obtained a copy of the Cicerone guide *Walking on Guernsey* can combine coastal walks around Guernsey, Alderney, Sark and Herm with a coastal walk around Jersey, thereby completing the 'Channel Islands Way' (see Appendix A). The full distance is around 178km (110 miles).

WALK 1
St Helier Town Trail

Distance	Variable
Terrain	Urban roads and pavements, as well as parks.
Start/Finish	Liberation Square, St Helier
Refreshments	Plenty of choice around St Helier.
Transport	All bus services on Jersey operate to and from Liberation Station.

St Helier is the largest town in Jersey and the Channel Islands, with several features of note. A rigid route description is hardly appropriate, and in fact there is no need to dedicate a whole day to a tour. Simply explore a different area of town any time you are passing through. There are so many places of interest, many of them apparent even if you are not particularly on the lookout for them. Lots of little plaques and memorials are fixed to all sorts of structures. The best approach is to visit the museum first, then explore some of the interesting streets and green spaces in town. Free town plans are easily obtained, and there is an excellent one on the back of the 1:25,000 Official Leisure Map of Jersey.

Within easy reach of the Weighbridge are three fine museums, all of which have entry charges.

The focal point for starting explorations around St Helier is the wide-open space around the Weighbridge, and, more precisely, **Liberation Square** and its striking bronze memorial. Carts laden with potatoes and other goods for shipment used to be weighed, then weighed again unladen at the Weighbridge. The difference between the two weights was the weight of the goods, for which payment would be made. ◄ The award-winning **Jersey Museum**, tel. 01534 633300, is in the Ordnance Yard. It explains all about Jersey's development from its most ancient bedrock to the flickering Reuters screens which offer constant news updates for the world of commerce and high finance.

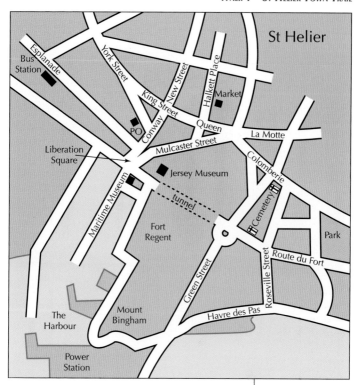

The **Maritime Museum**, tel. 01534 633372, is situated on the harbourside. It covers everything from the nature of the weather and tides to sea-life and the lives of fishermen and boat-builders, with plenty of hands-on exhibits. The museum also houses the Occupation Tapestry and details how it was made in the 12 parishes of Jersey.

There are several interesting streets clustered around the Weighbridge. The Esplanade no longer runs beside the sea, as harbour developments have pushed further and further seawards. Following the Esplanade launches straight into **Walk 2** around St Aubin's Bay. Both

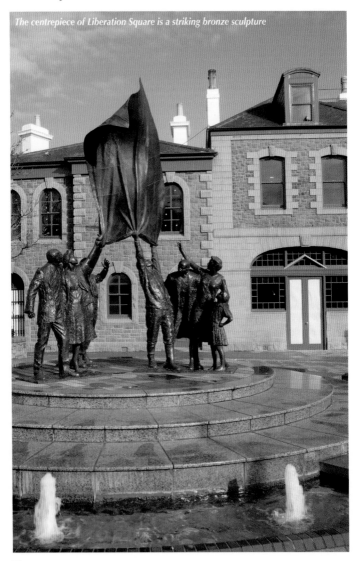

The centrepiece of Liberation Square is a striking bronze sculpture

Mulcaster Street and **Conway Street** lead directly from **Liberation Square** to the town centre, and both run close to the ancient Parish Church of St Helier.

If following **Conway Street**, a left turn leads onto Broad Street, where the head post office is located, and enquiries can be made about Jersey stamps and first day covers. There is onward access to **King Street**, **Queen Street**, **New Street** and other pedestrianised shopping streets. The old Market Hall, one of the busiest retail spaces in the Channel Islands, is an imposing building on **Halkett Place**.

Following Mulcaster Street from the Weighbridge leads to the States Offices, with access to Royal Square and its fine buildings.

The name **Peirson** is forever associated with this square, where the last pitched battle with French forces took place in 1781. Major Peirson won the day, but lost his life, as did the French leader Baron de Rullecourt (see the end of Walk 17 for more information).

By now, several tall buildings associated with commerce and high finance will have been noticed, and these now dominate the town centre.

Looking across the harbour towards the centre of St Helier, with Fort Regent rising to the right

An old cemetery is now managed as if it were a hay meadow, and around 100 species of plants grow in this little plot.

Also dominating the skyline, and named on many signposts, is **Fort Regent**. Although an old stone wall can be seen encircling this whaleback ridge, once enclosing a 19th century fort, the structures beyond are quite modern. Fort Regent is now a large and varied leisure centre full of attractions and entertainment. What appears to be a mast and rigging rising over the site is actually the last working signal station to be used in the British Isles.

There is no need to climb up to Fort Regent. Simply follow Hill Street and turn right onto Grenville Street to reach Green Street. ◄ Cutting through the **cemetery** leads to Hastings Road, which can be used to reach **Howard Davis Park**. This park is laid out quite formally,

The Parish Church of St Helier stands in the centre of the town

with lovely rose gardens, and is well used by locals and visitors. A memorial building tells the story behind the park.

Roads lead down to the sea and a slipway at Le Dicq. The road called **Havre des Pas** runs past modern developments, but in previous years the scene was quite different. Fort d'Auvergne once stood here and the area was notable for shipbuilding. ▶ When the tide is out, rocky reefs appear and careful seamanship is required to navigate around them. A promenade path can be followed round to La Collette, where barracks are surrounded by flowery gardens. La Collette Gardens rise steeply onto the wooded rise of **Mount Bingham**, which is all parkland and paths. The area also features a towering power station chimney, a prominent landmark.

Ships were constructed on the beaches and either floated off on the high tides, or launched from wooden slides.

Walking back into town via the harbour reveals much of interest. There are immense retaining walls above the Victoria, French and English Harbours. ▶ Close to hand are the Maritime Museum, Weighbridge, Jersey Museum and **Liberation Square**, so explorations have come full circle.

Seats around the Old Harbour carry the names of ships, leading to a curious Steam Clock.

There is so much to see around St Helier, so spend time pounding the streets looking for interesting plaques and monuments. Shops offer goods at duty-free prices, while restaurants offer a wide variety of food and drink. There are constant distractions and you can almost smell the money being made by the financial institutions. Behind St Helier's bustling facade is a town rich in history and heritage, waiting to be discovered. There are sometimes guided heritage walks around town and the tourist information centre can provide details of any taking place during your visit.

WALK 2
St Helier to St Aubin

Distance	5km (3 miles)
Terrain	A short, easy, firm promenade walk. Optional extensions along tidal causeways allow fortified islands to be visited.
Start	Liberation Square, St Helier
Finish	St Aubin's Harbour
Refreshments	Plenty of choice around St Helier and St Aubin, and along the promenade between them. Café at Elizabeth Castle.
Transport	Amphibious vehicles serve Elizabeth Castle at any state of the tide. All buses serve St Helier. Buses 12, 12a, 15 and the Blue Explorer link St Helier and St Aubin. *Le Petit Train* runs along the promenade between St Helier and St Aubin.

A walk around St Aubin's Bay is easily accomplished using a level promenade path, or a fine sandy beach when the tide is out. The bay is flanked by two small, stoutly fortified islands, which can be included in the walk if the tide allows. A thorough exploration of Elizabeth Castle might take half a day, but St Aubin's Fort is not open to visitors. A couple of cylindrical Jersey Towers are tucked away among built-up areas, and there is no shortage of places offering food and drink.

The centrepiece of the garden is a fountain rising around a bronze sculpture of humans and dolphins swimming together.

Start on Liberation Square in St Helier and follow the Esplanade past Liberation Station and Jersey Tourism. Cross a busy road to reach Les Jardins de la Mer. This supports bushes and maritime plants. ◀ A curious boat-shaped restaurant called La Frégate is passed. Amphibious vehicles operate from a slipway nearby to **Elizabeth Castle**. Note the stone plaques set into the sea wall, recording the endeavours of round-the-island swimmers over the years.

Extension to Elizabeth Castle

Visiting Elizabeth Castle depends on the time and tide. When the tide is out, walkers can follow a concrete causeway across the sands. This spends more time underwater than it does out of the water, so check the tide times. Two blue amphibious vehicles, *Charming Betty* and *Charming Nancy*, operate regular bus/ferry services to and from Elizabeth Castle. Walking to the castle, around the castle, and back again, is an extra 4km (2½ miles).

When the tide is in and the causeway flooded, DUKW vehicles are used to reach Elizabeth Castle

Exploring Elizabeth Castle involves entering the Main Gate, where there is an entry charge, to look around Fort Charles and the Outer Ward. After continuing through the Lower Ward to the Upper Ward, amazing views encompass the whole site. It is also possible to walk along a stout breakwater to reach The Hermitage on a rocky islet. There are plenty of steps to climb up and down, and so many nooks and crannies to explore that the rest of the day could pass unnoticed. Several buildings contain military exhibits and displays, and there is a café.

History and heritage are jumbled together from one end of Elizabeth Castle to the other. St Helier's crude cave

41

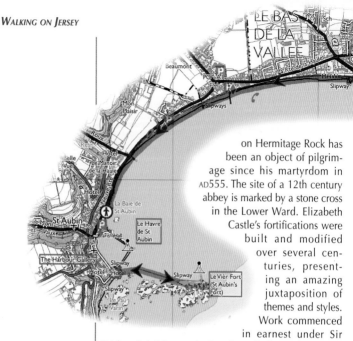

on Hermitage Rock has been an object of pilgrimage since his martyrdom in AD555. The site of a 12th century abbey is marked by a stone cross in the Lower Ward. Elizabeth Castle's fortifications were built and modified over several centuries, presenting an amazing juxtaposition of themes and styles. Work commenced in earnest under Sir Walter Raleigh, continuing through the 17th century. Several buildings form fine museums in their own right. Crowning the highest point is a German fire control tower, offering a bird's-eye view of the whole site. A gun platform was constructed there in 1550 when the island was first fortified. A cannon is fired at noon every day 'by the Grace of God'. Tel. 01534 633376 (castle), or 01534 634048 (ferry), www.jerseyheritage.org.

The Jersey Railway & Tramway Company opened a line along the promenade in 1870, which was dismantled in 1946.

Continue along the promenade, following a granite-paved path on top of the sea wall. Running parallel is a cycleway, and also watch out for *Le Petit Train*, which runs between St Helier and St Aubin. ◄ Keep in lane to avoid other users, and hope they have the same consideration for you! One of Jersey's busiest roads runs parallel, but there is no need to set foot on it.

The promenade walk is equipped with shelters, cafés, kiosks, toilets, seating and showers. When the First

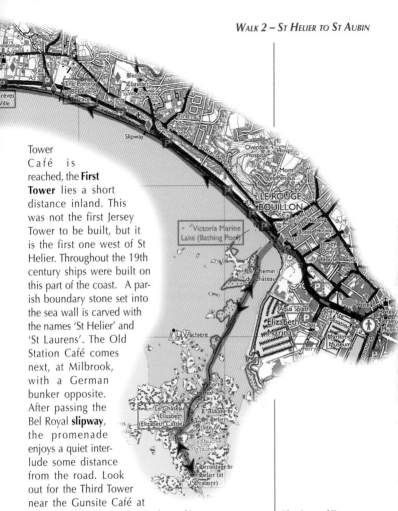

Tower Café is reached, the **First Tower** lies a short distance inland. This was not the first Jersey Tower to be built, but it is the first one west of St Helier. Throughout the 19th century ships were built on this part of the coast. A parish boundary stone set into the sea wall is carved with the names 'St Helier' and 'St Laurens'. The Old Station Café comes next, at Milbrook, with a German bunker opposite. After passing the Bel Royal **slipway**, the promenade enjoys a quiet interlude some distance from the road. Look out for the Third Tower near the Gunsite Café at **Beaumont**. ▶ After passing the café, catamarans are often drawn up beside the promenade. A small area of farmland is passed at **La Haule**, a break from the built-up flanks of the bay. Jersey Sea Sport Centre hires out equipment further along the promenade, and **St Aubin** is reached soon afterwards. This busy village offers a full

The Second Tower no longer exists; it was demolished during the German Occupation.

43

Catamarans are often drawn up onto the sands at Beaumont

To continue walking round the coast of Jersey refer to Walk 3, though it is also possible to continue straight along Walk 24 to La Corbière.

range of services, despite its small size. The walk can be finished here, using either buses or *Le Petit Train* to return to St Helier from the Salle Paroissiale de St Brelade. This was once the Terminus Hotel and railway station, and was rebuilt after being destroyed by fire in 1936. ◄

Extension to St Aubin's Fort

Visiting St Aubin's Fort depends on the time and tide. When the tide is out, a clear, firm, concrete causeway can be followed across the sands. To find this, walk beside St Aubin's Harbour to reach the Royal Channel Islands Yacht Club. A slipway descends to the sands and the causeway leads straight to St Aubin's Fort. It is possible to step onto the island, but the fort itself cannot be visited. The fort may be teeming with youngsters as it is managed by the Jersey Youth Service as an Outdoor Pursuits Centre.

The **fort** was built in the 1540s, when St Aubin's Harbour was the principal harbour on Jersey. The harbour at St Helier was completed as late as the 1840s. Interestingly, before the development of Jersey Airport, small aircraft used to land on the sands of St Aubin's Bay and pay harbour dues!

WALK 3
Noirmont Point and Ouaisné

Distance	12km (7½ miles)
Terrain	Fine woodland and headland paths, with 'green lanes' inland.
Start/Finish	St Aubin's Harbour
Refreshments	Plenty of choice in St Aubin and at St Brelade's Bay. Pubs and cafés are available at Portelet and Ouaisné.
Transport	Buses 12, 12a, 15 and the Blue Explorer serve St Aubin from St Helier. Bus 12 links St Brelade's Bay and St Aubin, 12a also serves the Old Portelet Inn and the Blue Explorer serves all those places. *Le Petit Train* runs along the promenade from St Helier to St Aubin.

Noirmont Point and Portelet Common, south of St Aubin and St Brelade, are surrounded by rocky cliffs and rugged slopes. Noirmont was heavily fortified during the German Occupation and overlooks St Helier and Portelet Bay. Other features of interest include a cave at La Cotte de St Brelade where the bones of mammoth and woolly rhinoceros were discovered. An important wetland nature reserve is located nearby at Ouaisné. All these places can be tied together in a circuit which is easy, interesting and varied.

High water at St Aubin's Harbour. At low water the harbour is completely dry

45

ST AUBIN

St Aubin's Harbour is full of moored vessels, but dries completely at low water. From the 16th century this was the safest harbour on Jersey, but it declined in importance following the 19th century development of the harbour at St Helier. Today St Aubin is a bustling place full of pubs and restaurants. A curious stone carving on the wall of the NatWest Bank begs *Souvenez-vous les pauvres* (Remember the poor)! The Salle Paroissiale de St Brelade, was once the Terminus Hotel and railway station, and now houses the police station.

Leave **St Aubin** by walking along the harbourside. The road climbs inland from the Royal Channel Islands Yacht Club and is called Mont du Boulevard. It twists and turns to pass the Somerville Hotel and becomes a 'green lane' called Mont ès Tours, flanked by tall trees and flowery banks. The road levels out among fields and is called Rue de Haut, reaching a junction with the busier Route de Noirmont at **Les Bailhaches**.

Turn left to follow the road through a crossroads. Just afterwards, on the left, is a footpath sign. Keep left while following the path, always with a fence to the left, through mixed woods. There are plenty of other paths that could be explored on another visit. The trees thin out later, giving way to gorse, brambles, bracken, heather and plenty of flowers. After passing crumbling granite boulders, concrete bunkers and gun emplacements can be seen around **Noirmont**, and there is a road-end car park.

COMMAND BUNKER AND OBSERVATION TOWER

The *Batterie Lothringen* complex sprawls among gorse bushes at the top of Noirmont. German forces expended an immense amount of labour building huge concrete structures, which extend deep into the granite rock. Most of the buildings were bomb-proof and gas-proof, controlling huge guns which were only rarely fired. Channel Island Occupation Society guides are sometimes on hand to take visitors around both the bunker and tower, which contain interesting models, exhibits and supporting literature. Opening times are limited and there is an entry charge, www.ciosjersey.org.uk.

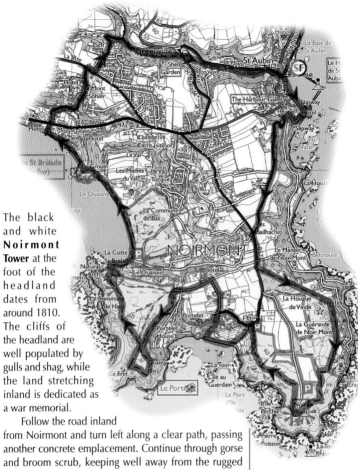

The black and white **Noirmont Tower** at the foot of the headland dates from around 1810. The cliffs of the headland are well populated by gulls and shag, while the land stretching inland is dedicated as a war memorial.

Follow the road inland from Noirmont and turn left along a clear path, passing another concrete emplacement. Continue through gorse and broom scrub, keeping well away from the rugged cliffs. The path leads to a point overlooking Portelet Bay and L'Île au Guerdain. Walk towards the nearest house in view, keeping right of it to reach a car park and bus stop at **Portelet**. Turn left to reach the nearby Old Portelet Inn, which was established in 1606.

If the tide is fully in and covers the beach at Portelet, then follow a narrow road towards an area of new apartments, turning right to reach the Portelet Hotel. If the tide is out, then walk down concrete steps from the Old

47

L'Île au Guerdain, or Janvrin's Tomb, can be visited at low water from the beach below Portelet

Mesembryanthemum drapes the cliffs around the bay.

Portelet Inn to the beach. ◄ Turn right along the beach to reach a derelict café or, if the tide allows, walk onto **L'Île au Guerdain**, locally known as Janvrin's Tomb.

In 1721 a local seafarer, Philippe Janvrin, died of the plague while at sea. Jersey folk wouldn't allow the body ashore, but permitted a burial on **L'Île au Guerdain**. The body was later exhumed and re-interred at St Brelade's. Portelet Tower, the Martello Tower that crowns the island, dates from 1808.

Climb up steps from the derelict café, passing apartments to climb more steps. Continue straight ahead by road to reach the **Portelet Hotel**. Turn left along a narrow road, passing a few houses to approach a small car park on the Portelet Common nature reserve. Turn left just before the car park, as signposted 'footpath', following a track with a fence to the left. Tall pines grow on the seaward slope to the left, while holm oaks grow to the right.

A metal gateway is reached in a stone wall. Go through it to enjoy a fine short circular walk around a granite headland. Trees give way to gorse and heather, while rugged cliffs drop to the sea. Come back through the gate and follow the wall onwards, approaching a solitary whitewashed cottage. Don't go all the way to the cottage, which stands above **La Cotte de St Brelade**.

LA COTTE DE ST BRELADE

This cave is out of sight and also out of bounds to visitors. Palaeolithic nomads used the cave over 200,000 years ago, and Neanderthal human remains from 75,000 years ago have also been retrieved, from a time when Jersey was part of the European mainland, rising as low hills above a plain. Mammoths and woolly rhinoceros were driven over the cliffs, then butchered and eaten. Fortunately for posterity, their bones were stashed inside the cave, where they were discovered by archaeologists. The site was deemed so important that work ceased and the cave was sealed, pending a more thorough investigation. The Jersey Museum in St Helier and La Hougue Bie Museum contain some of the bones and artefacts from the site.

Walk along the cliff tops, away from the cottage, until a path drops down wooden steps through an old quarry. Ivy creeps over the granite faces, and lichen softens angular breaks in the rock. A very high tide might bar the way to Ouaisné for a few minutes, otherwise it is simply a matter of walking to a slipway and coming ashore beside The Beach House restaurant. ▶ A notice in a car park explains about the **Ouaisné Common** nature reserve.

The Old Smugglers Inn, dating from 1721, lies further inland.

Ouaisné Common is an area of wetland and dry heath held behind a concrete sea wall. It is a refuge for uncommon birds, such as the Dartford warbler.

49

The agile frog and toads are resident, as are green lizards and grass snakes. A stout Jersey Tower of 1780 is painted red and white as a navigation marker.

Walk along the top of the sea wall or along the beach if the tide is out. Pass the Jersey Tower and a concrete bunker. Cross a wooded point called **Le Grouin** and descend, keeping left at a junction, onto a concrete promenade path. This can be followed all the way into St Brelade, where it is possible to catch a bus. ◄ To explore inland, just walk to the outskirts of the village, to the Wayside Café near a Jersey Tower, and turn right along a narrow road.

To continue walking round the coast of Jersey, refer to Walk 4.

St Brelade's Bay is full of hotels, pubs, restaurants and cafés, but has other features of interest too. St Brelade's Parish Church and Fishermen's Chapel are well worth visiting. Just above the promenade is a beautiful garden, while across the road is the Sir Winston Churchill Memorial Park. The site includes an artificial waterfall, while paths wind up a steep slope to reach Red Houses.

Walking inland from the Wayside Café, cross the main road and walk up a 'green lane' called Mont Gras d'Eau. Climb past the Château des Roches, reaching the **Hotel Miramar** before joining a busy road. Turn right along this, then take the second left, a 'green lane' called Mont Nicolle. ◄ The road runs down into a valley and makes a pronounced right turn, heading for **Greenville**. Go under a bridge and turn right up a few steps to get onto the Corbière Walk, an old railway track-bed followed on **Walk 24**.

Do not take the road to the school also called Mont Nicolle.

Turn left to follow the track-bed gently downhill with woods alongside. Go under a stone arch carrying a busy road, and later cross a minor road beside a stout stone marker. Continue down the track-bed to reach a road-end, and follow the road quickly down into **St Aubin**, finishing beside the harbour.

WALK 4

St Brelade's Bay and La Corbière

Distance	10km (6¼ miles)
Terrain	Rugged cliff paths, with some easier tracks. An optional tidal causeway can be followed to La Corbière lighthouse.
Start/Finish	St Brelade's Bay
Refreshments	Plenty of choice at St Brelade's Bay. Pubs and restaurants are available at La Corbière and La Pulente, and a tea house at La Moye.
Transport	Bus 12 links St Brelade and La Corbière, 12a serves La Pulente and the Blue Explorer serves all those places.

The extreme south-west coast of Jersey has some striking cliff scenery and several points of interest. Coastal paths and tracks, with some diversions inland, allow a fine walk from St Brelade's Bay to La Corbière. When the tide is out a concrete causeway allows walkers to reach the rocky islet of La Corbière, which is crowned by a striking lighthouse. Coastal walkers can continue beyond La Corbière and La Pulente, around St Ouen's Bay, while others may return inland to St Brelade's Bay.

Leave St Brelade's Bay by walking through the grounds of St Brelade's Parish Church. Leave via the top gate and turn left along a road signposted 'Footpath to Beauport'. At the top of a steep uphill stretch, a granite block on the right indicates the way to Beauport Bay. Follow a path that twists and turns up a wooded slope, then climbs steeply between gorse bushes, levelling out beside fields. The path is often crunchy with pulverised granite and it leads to a car park, where a notice explains about **Les Creux** Millennium Country Park. ▸

Walk in front of the car park and keep high along the tops of the cliffs, enjoying fine views back across Beauport Bay to St Brelade and Portelet Common. The

A path drops down a steep slope of bracken to a sandy beach at Beauport Bay, which is flanked by granite headlands. If the bay is visited, climb back afterwards.

ST BRELADE'S PARISH CHURCH

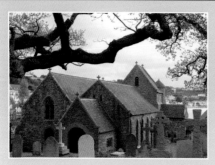

St Brelade was the son of a Cornish king. He might have visited Jersey and founded a church, but nothing is known for certain. The parish church has been extended several times from the 12th century, without causing much architectural conflict. Most of the granite is rough, with only a few dressed stones and columns. The vaulted granite roof and arches are amazing. Outside, note the number of Greek crosses on the gables, and the lovely little *tourelle*, or round tower. The Fishermen's Chapel is an unevenly shaped building with remarkable frescoes inside, dating from the 14th and 15th centuries. Outside, a gateway bears a sign announcing the *perquage*, or sanctuary path to the shore, which could be taken by any person being banished from Jersey after committing a serious crime, provided they reached the sanctuary of the church before being caught.

path is good, flanked by gorse scrub and flowers, but there are several other paths in the area. After passing a stout marker stone for **La Grosse Tête**, one of these paths makes a short loop around an impressive rocky headland. Afterwards, another marker stone indicates the coastal path heading off to the left. It crosses slopes of gorse, bracken and brambles, passing seawards of a large and a smaller house. Drop down steps into a dip, then climb steps up a steep slope. At the top of the cliff there is a concrete bunker to the left.

The path is later diverted inland from the cliffs at the Old Signal Point, and a narrow road runs around a corner of a tall fence bounding Jersey's prison. A footpath signpost points to the left, indicating a stony track across **La Lande du Ouest** Site of Special Interest. The track reaches a curious tall tower – a meteorological radar station. Keep right of it then turn left to follow a path back towards the cliffs. A broad moorland slope features gorse, broom and heather. ▶ There is a slight move inland to pass two houses, then the path continues along the cliffs before descending steps to pass below a **desalination plant**. Climb beside an inclined narrow-gauge railway line and turn left at the top.

The cliff path turns a rocky headland and approaches the prominent **Highlands Hotel**. A recent re-routing keeps the path high, but the old convoluted path can be followed down towards a bouldery beach at **La Rosière**. ▶ Walk onto the next headland to reach a prominent German observation tower, which is let as holiday accommodation by Jersey Heritage, www. jerseyheritage.org/heritage-holiday-lets. There are fine views of La Corbière lighthouse, while Le Nid de Corneilles offers food and drink nearby. There are buses and toilets, with access to the Corbière Walk, described in **Walk 24**.

This is a good area for bird watching, and offers a chance to spot Dartford warbler, cirl bunting and serin.

Note a granite-paved path round the base of the cliff, leading to an interesting cave. If this is followed, take care when the tide is high, and retrace your steps afterwards.

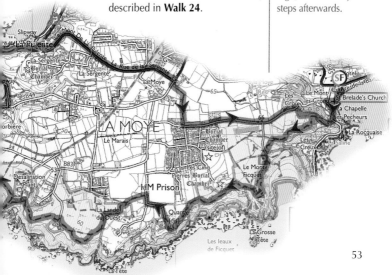

Two nearby **concrete bunkers** are sometimes open for inspection when Channel Island Occupation Society guides are on hand. One is a mortar bunker, while the other is a coastal defence gun casemate. There is an entry charge, **www.ciosjersey.org.uk**.

Extension to La Corbière Lighthouse
Visiting La Corbière depends on the time and tide. When the tide is out, a clear, firm, concrete causeway can be followed. This spends more time underwater than out of the water. To reach the causeway, walk down a narrow road, passing a 'helping hand' sculpture. The start of the causeway is flanked by warning signs. Read them carefully, and note the memorial to a lighthouse keeper who drowned trying to save a stranded visitor. The causeway runs easily across jagged, low-lying granite. The rocky islet of La Corbière can be gained, but there is no access to the lighthouse, so retrace your steps back across the causeway to continue. A siren sounds when the tide is advancing. The walk there and back is 1.5km (1 mile).

At low water a tidal causeway allows the walk to be extended to a lighthouse at La Corbière

LA CORBIÈRE LIGHTHOUSE

The rocks around La Corbière have wrecked many ships, and the lighthouse was constructed here in 1873. The little white tower was the first concrete lighthouse to be erected in the world and in fair weather it is a notable landmark. A plaque on the causeway outlines its design and specifications. The granite 'helping hand' sculpture at the top of the access road commemorates the rescue of 307 passengers and crew from the French catamaran ferry 'St Malo', which hit nearby rocks in April 1995.

Follow the main road downhill, slicing twice through granite outcrops at Roche Mouette, passing a few buildings. Pass one junction, where a road comes in from the left, and walk straight ahead following the road across a rugged and well-vegetated slope. Turn left down the short Chemin du Petit Port, reaching a granite slipway at **Le Petit Port**. Pick up a path climbing granite steps above the **slipway** and retaining wall, on a slope of gorse. Turn left along a clearer, gentler path. Note an old quarry to the right and a bunker to the left. La Pulente comes into sight, offering food and drink. ▸

To continue walking round the coast of Jersey, follow a path parallel to the road to La Pulente, then refer to Walk 5.

There is a bus stop at **La Pulente**, if the walk is to be cut short, otherwise walk up the busy road to return inland to St Brelade's Bay. Take care on a blind bend, and at the top of **Mont de La Pulente**, use the gritty pavement beside the road, crossing the Corbière Walk (**Walk 24**), to reach a junction with another busy road at **La Moye**.

Turn right, then immediately left, along a farm track called Oak Lane. This bends right as it passes a few fields, reaching a junction with a road. Turn left to follow the road past houses, then through fields. Paths indicated by stone markers allow an exploration of Les Creux Millennium Country Park, passed at the start of the walk. Watch out for a stone marked 'St Brelade's Church' on the right. Follow a path and keep left, linking with the first footpath used at the start of the day's walk. Simply follow this, and a road, downhill to return to St Brelade's Bay.

WALK 5
La Pulente and Les Quennevais

Distance	5km (3 miles)
Terrain	Sandy and grassy paths over dunes, with some woodland paths too. Short stretches on woodland paths can sometimes be muddy.
Start/Finish	La Pulente
Refreshments	Restaurants at La Pulente and a café at Le Braye.
Transport	Bus 12a and the Blue Explorer serve La Pulente and Le Braye.

The southern part of St Ouen's Bay is backed by the extensive dunes of Les Blanches Banques, part of the 'special' area of Les Mielles, designated in 1978 as a sort of 'trainee national park'. It is a popular area where there is a need to balance conservation and recreation. The dunes are home to hundreds of species of plants, and feature a handful of ancient monuments. The whole area is criss-crossed with sandy paths, so the following route steers its way through with reference to strong navigational features.

La Pulente has a bus service, car park, toilets, and a couple of restaurants. Follow the path beside the sea wall around the broad sweep of St Ouen's Bay, or if the tides permit, walk along the sandy beach. The shore path crosses a concrete bunker. This is sometimes open to visitors when Channel Island Occupation Society members are present, and there is an entry charge, www.ciosjersey.org.uk. Beyond the bunker, the path continues through the dunes, but if walking along the beach, come ashore at a prominent slipway at **Le Braye**, where there is a café, car park and toilets. Whichever route is chosen, **La Rocco Tower** is a prominent feature offshore. ◄

To continue walking round the coast of Jersey, follow the beach or sea wall past beach cafés and restaurants, then refer to Walk 6.

La Rocco Tower, built in 1795, can be visited at low water while walking round St Ouen's Bay

LA ROCCO TOWER

If the tide is a long way out, it is possible to make a short visit to lonely La Rocco Tower. This was built on a rocky islet in 1795, guarding the southern part of St Ouen's Bay. It is a typical Jersey Tower, the last of its type to be built, featuring an additional gun platform round its base. Martello Towers were later built around the bay. La Rocco Tower suffered extensive damage during the German Occupation, when troops used it for target practice. It was in danger of complete collapse but was restored in the 1970s.

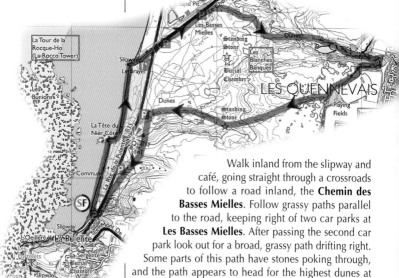

Walk inland from the slipway and café, going straight through a crossroads to follow a road inland, the **Chemin des Basses Mielles**. Follow grassy paths parallel to the road, keeping right of two car parks at **Les Basses Mielles**. After passing the second car park look out for a broad, grassy path drifting right. Some parts of this path have stones poking through, and the path appears to head for the highest dunes at **Les Blanches Banques**. In fact, the path bears left and climbs through a shallow valley to exploit a gap in the dunes. ◄ If the gap is crossed at the right point, a pool of water is seen on the right, with dense woodland beyond.

As height is gained, views back towards the sea reveal only La Rocco Tower.

Keep left of the pool and follow the clearest path into the wooded valley. The woods quickly become quite dense, with a rich jungle-like understorey. ▶ There is a network of paths, and by climbing up any clear path to the right, a fence will be reached which encloses a sports pitch. This is part of Les Quennevais Sports Centre. Turn right to folj64low paths parallel to the fence, turning left round a corner of the fence later. A small plantation of pine trees are reached, where a fence running right marks the boundary of La Moye Golf Course. ▶

Walk parallel to the boundary fence of the golf course, but gradually drift away from it. The dunes are mostly quite stable and well vegetated, even bearing clumps of shrubs in places, but some parts are soft and sandy. Views are quite extensive, and when there is a clear view down to the sea, look out for a prominent standing stone in a broad, grassy area dotted with trees. This provides a useful guide on the way down towards the coast road. Don't go all the way to the road, but turn left and pass a car park near the road.

A flight of wooden steps climbs from the car park, past a concrete bunker onto a rocky promontory. This provides a good vantage point for enjoying the view; then

This is known locally as the 'Creepy Valley', a name now used by an adventure centre in the woods.

A path through the pines, between the sports centre and golf course, links with the Corbière Walk, Walk 24.

The sand dunes near La Moye are well vegetated but feature occasional sandy blow-outs

walk down the other side and head for another car park. **La Pulente** is just a short walk beyond.

LES BLANCHES BANQUES

The dunes of Les Blanches Banques are 3000 to 4000 years old. Although the area was settled in Neolithic times, it is uninhabited today. The dunes are stable and support a rich and varied range of plants. Some 400 species have been recorded, including Mediterranean plants at their northernmost limits. Green lizards and an abundance of insects can also be seen. Areas are fenced in early summer to provide safe habitats for ground-nesting skylarks. Les Blanches Banques is the fourth richest sand dune system in Europe in terms of its flora, and the area is a designated Nature Conservation Zone. In some areas erosion of the dunes has been halted by planting with marram grass; in other places gorse and tree scrub have been cleared to increase the range of vegetation. Rare plants in danger of disappearing include sand crocus, fragrant evening primrose, great sea stock and dwarf pansy. The natural history of Les Mielles can be studied at the Kempt Tower Interpretation Centre at the northern end of St Ouen's Bay (see **Walk 6**).

A pool of water is hidden from sight and only seen at close quarters on Les Blanches Banques

WALK 6
Les Mielles and St Ouen

Distance	8km (5 miles)
Terrain	Easy paths, tracks and roads across heaths, through woods, beside a reservoir and along the coast.
Start/Finish	Kempt Tower, Les Mielles
Refreshments	A beach café is available towards the end.
Transport	Bus 12a and the Blue Explorer pass Kempt Tower.

At its fullest extent Les Mielles stretch around St Ouen's Bay from La Pulente to Le Grand Étacquerel, and as far inland as the steep slopes that rise from the lower dunes and fields. Some parts were exploited for sand, and deep holes were used as landfill sites in the 1970s. Wonderful restoration work has been accomplished since that time. The area was designated as a 'special' place in 1978 in an effort to control development and recreation in a way that would help to preserve and enhance the natural environment. This walk is based on the Kempt Tower Interpretation Centre and includes the coast and heaths, valleys and farmland around St Ouen's Bay.

Kempt Tower, a Martello tower, was built in 1834 and serves as the interpretation centre for Les Mielles conservation area. There is an entry charge and opening

Kempt Tower, built in 1834, serves as a visitor centre for Les Mielles

61

times are limited to a few hours in the afternoons. The interior is a doughnut-shaped space around a brick column, with a curved ceiling. There are two levels and a range of splendid displays. There is access to the roof, a fine viewpoint that once supported a cannon.

Across the road is a nature reserve, and nearby is the Frances Le Sueur Centre, a base for environmental organisations.

Leave Kempt Tower and cross the road to enter a car park. Turn left to walk parallel to the road, passing a reedy pool where there are a couple of bird hides. Go round the back of two houses to reach a track. Turn right inland, following a path parallel to the track. The track ends on **La Mielle de Morville**, where a network of paths is available.

LA MIELLE DE MORVILLE

Uncommon birds in the area include the Dartford warbler, Cetti's warbler, cirl bunting and serin. Birds more commonly spotted include sand martin, swallow, reed warbler, great tit, coot, moorhen, tufted duck, water rail, snipe and kingfisher. Kestrels may be seen hovering in search of prey. The wetland areas are home to the agile frog, while the green lizard and great green bush cricket might also be noticed. Some 200 species of flowering plants include the burnet rose, spotted orchid and purple viper's bugloss. The broad sands of St Ouen's Bay feature a variety of waders, with enormous seasonal variations in numbers and species.

To continue, follow a path rising gently, reaching a narrow road. Cross the road and continue along a track, rising gradually through fields towards higher ground. Turn left onto a narrower track, which becomes a clear bramble-banked path leading towards a house and garden. Follow the path up into a valley, which gradually becomes more wooded. Note a path on the right, maintained by the Rotary Club. Emerge on a narrow tarmac road at **La Ville au Bas**, overlooking a small pool behind an old reservoir dam. Turn right and keep right, following Rue de Couvent, a 'green lane', then keep to the left where it is marked 'no through road'. This leads to a gate giving access to **St Ouen's Church**, which is well worth a visit.

ST OUEN'S PARISH CHURCH

The foundation date is unknown, but there may have been a church on this site from the 6th century. The list of rectors stretches back to 1156 and the church is certainly much older. Stout pillars and stonework feature inside, and a study of styles indicates that the building has grown through the centuries and the church has been considerably altered. There are some quite old pieces of stonework in the churchyard, including some interesting monuments to past preachers. St Ouen was born around the year 609. He was a court official before becoming a bishop and is associated especially with Rouen. He died near Paris in the year 684.

Le Val de la Mare Reservoir has a path running all the way round its shoreline

Leave the church by way of the main gate and walk straight along La Rue. Turn right at the bottom to walk along Mont Rossignol, past fields and houses, and look out for a sign on the left for **Le Val de la Mare Reservoir**. Keep to the left-hand track over a scrubby rise. Go through a small gate on the left and walk down concrete and wooden steps to reach the reservoir shore. Turn right to follow the shoreline path to the dam. ◄

Walk 23 uses a path on the opposite shore.

Drop down steps beside the dam to reach a lower track, which leads to a gateway, car park and road. Turn right along the road, then left at a crossroads, following a 'green lane' called Route de la Marette. The road turns left and right past a field owned by the National Trust for Jersey, then passes **Les Mielles Golf and Country Club**. A menhir might be spotted on the golf course to the right before reaching the clubhouse. ◄ At the end of the road is a driving range and a laser pigeon range.

The menhir used to be whitewashed.

Cross the main road and aim for St Ouen's Bay. Turn right to follow the sea wall past a large building. Next is a small guardhouse, built in 1765, owned by the National Trust for Jersey, called La Caumine à Marie Best.

(The guardhouse offers very basic accommodation.)The Surf Shop beside a **slipway** offers food and drink, with a concrete bunker alongside. Pass **La Tour Carrée**, built in 1778, now painted black and white as a navigational aid. After passing a house called The Cutty Sark, the walk ends back at the **Kempt Tower**. ▶

To continue walking round the coast of Jersey, follow the beach or sea wall to Lewis Tower to link with Walk 7.

ST OUEN'S BAY FORTIFICATIONS

During the German Occupation St Ouen's Bay was seen as a weak point and an impressive number of fortifications was constructed. A sea wall was constructed round the broad sweep of the bay, overlooked by coastal batteries, supplemented by concrete bunkers and more weaponry along its length. Thousands of mines were laid and a ditch was dug as a tank trap. Further inland, at the top of the steep slopes above the bay, there were even more strong points containing an array of weapons. This whole system of coastal fortifications was controlled from a bunker far inland at St Peter's village.

Picking potatoes near the end of the walk

WALK 7

L'Étacq and Plémont

Distance	11km (7 miles)
Terrain	Easy coastal paths and minor roads.
Start/Finish	Lewis Tower, near L'Étacq
Refreshments	Restaurants available near Lewis Tower, seafood takeaway at Le Grand Étacquerel, café at Plémont and a tearoom/bistro at Portinfer.
Transport	Bus 12a and the Red and Blue Explorers serve Lewis Tower. Bus 12a and the Red Explorer serve L'Étacq. Buses 7b and 8 serve Plémont in summer, and 8 serves Portinfer.

A popular coastal walk runs round the north-western corner of Jersey, from L'Étacq to Grosnez Castle and Plémont. There are bus services at either end, but it is worth completing a circuit by following roads back inland, discovering lush, fertile Jersey farmland. The crossroads village of Portinfer is passed and a series of narrow lanes can be followed around Les Ruettes to return to the coast. Visitor attractions at the start and finish include Jersey Pearl and the Channel Islands Military Museum. Lewis Tower is in the same area of Les Mielles as the Channel Islands Military Museum and Jersey Pearl. Visit these sites at the beginning of the walk, or save them until the end.

CHANNEL ISLANDS MILITARY MUSEUM

The Military Museum is housed in a large concrete bunker, open daily March to October, and there is an entry charge. It was one of over 60 sites constructed during the German Occupation to defend St Ouen's Bay, along with minefields stretching from L'Étacq to La Pulente. The thick-walled underground rooms are filled with models in uniform, small vehicles, artefacts and memorabilia from the Occupation. There are taped commentaries featuring sound-bites from those years. The bunker was built into the sea wall next to Lewis Tower, which was a Martello tower built around 1835. The Germans adapted the tower and incorporated it into their defences. A similar tower at L'Étacquerel was demolished and replaced with a bunker.

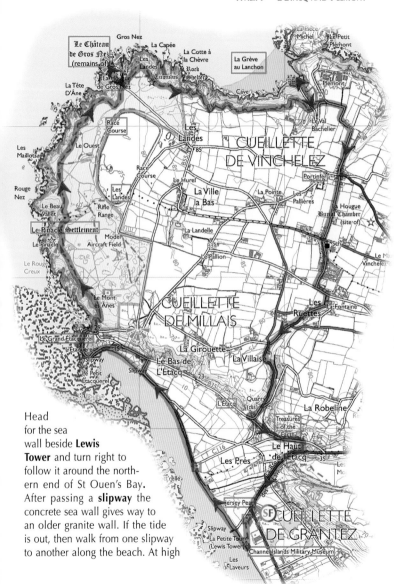

Head
for the sea
wall beside **Lewis
Tower** and turn right to
follow it around the northern end of St Ouen's Bay.
After passing a **slipway** the
concrete sea wall gives way to
an older granite wall. If the tide
is out, then walk from one slipway
to another along the beach. At high

Le Pinacle dominates the site of an ancient settlement and is a striking landmark

tide, follow the road inland to **Le Bas de L'Étacq** and turn left for **Le Grand Étacquerel**. The road round the headland has a car park and bus service, while a prominent concrete bunker now houses a seafood takeaway.

Follow the road, Route des Havres, uphill and avoid a turning to the shore. Watch out for a path on the left signposted 'Cliffpath to Grosnez'. Steps zigzag up a rugged, flowery slope onto gorse and granite to reach the broad upland heaths of **Les Landes** Site of Special Interest. Concrete bunkers and gun emplacements are dotted around, all part of the *Batterie Möltke* constructed during the German Occupation. Some of the big guns have been salvaged and repositioned after being dumped over the cliffs. Further along, in a rugged natural coastal amphitheatre, a monstrous rock called **Le Pinacle** overlooks the site of an early settlement.

Les Landes is the largest of Jersey's maritime heaths, on an exposed cliff-top with very poor soil, but there is a variety of plants and animals. Some 200 species of plant thrive in this open environment, as well as several species of dragonfly and butterfly. The Jersey bank vole and Dartford warbler have been recorded. Birds of prey include sparrowhawk, hen harrier, merlin and peregrine. Further inland there is a race course and a model aircraft airfield.

A tall German observation tower is seen further along the cliffs and is soon reached. There may be views across the sea to Sark, Herm and Guernsey. A lovely cliff coast follows, resplendent with flowers, and after crossing a little valley the ruins of **Grosnez Castle** can be seen. Beyond its gateway, concrete steps lead down to a small signal station where there are splendid cliff coast views, but retrace your steps afterwards.

Concrete steps lead from Grosnez Castle to a small signal station affording fine cliff views

GROSNEZ CASTLE

Occupying a headland in the extreme north-west of Jersey, Grosnez Castle was built in the 14th century to provide a refuge during frequent French attacks. Farmers and fishermen in the north-west of Jersey were usually alerted to raids by the ringing of church bells. The gatehouse features a series of ditches cut into the rock, which were spanned by a drawbridge. An excavation found traces of six buildings inside the main castle wall, though there was no evidence of a well. It is known that by 1540 the castle was in ruins.

Leave the castle to pass a car park and a quarry, then follow a path further round the cliffs, passing heather and

Grosnez Castle, built in the 14th century, was essentially a refuge for people in north-west Jersey

The beach can only be reached by descending flights of steps from a cliff café.

gorse. The headland of La Tête de Plémont comes into view, with the point of Ronez visible far beyond. The cliffs feature jagged fangs and overhangs, and the beach at **Plémont** is surrounded by cliffs. ◄ Walk down steps, cross a stream and a road in a little valley above the café, then climb steps to a car park. There is a summer bus terminus here, allowing the walk to be cut short, otherwise head inland by road. ◄

To continue walking round the coast of Jersey, follow the cliff path onwards, referring to Walk 8.

Follow the Route de Plémont inland to **Portinfer**. This crossroads village has a tearoom/bistro and bus service. Continue straight along Rue de la Porte to a crossroads at **St George's Church**, and continue along Rue des Cosnets past Les Landes School. Turn left along Rue à la Pendue, then right, passing La Fontaine, a house bearing a plaque in memory of Louisa Mary Gould.

The **plaque** reads 'In this house Mrs Louisa Mary Gould, née Le Druillenec, sheltered an escaped Russian POW during the German Occupation from October 1942 until May 1944. After her arrest she was deported to the concentration camp at Ravensbruck where she perished in the gas chamber.'

Turn right at the next junction at **Les Ruettes** to follow a road called Le Mont, along and down into a little valley full of farms and houses. Keep straight on at La Ruette, but turn left at a crossroads, down Mont Huëlin. At the bottom of the valley, beside an old quarry, turn left to walk into the little village of **Le Haut de l'Étacq**. Pass a shop and gallery called Treasure Earth, which has amazing displays of crystals and fossils.

After passing Treasure Earth, turn right and right again through a car park to follow another road downhill from Les Prés d'Auvergne. The road turns a corner around Jersey Pearl, leading to The Château, the Channel Islands Military Museum and Lewis Tower. If these places were not visited at the start of the walk, they can be explored while waiting for the next bus.

JERSEY PEARL

Jersey Pearl is an interesting place to visit. A large showroom is dedicated to the display and sale of pearl-based jewellery. There are also notes and displays explaining all about natural, cultured and artificial pearls. A replica of the world's largest pearl sits in an enormous clam shell, while a pearl dress modelled on one worn by Princess Diana is also on display. You can pick your own pearl from an oyster, but it may not be quite so big! There is a café on site.

WALK 8
Plémont and La Grève de Lecq

Distance	8km (5 miles)
Terrain	Cliff paths with flights of steps, followed by quiet roads through an agricultural landscape.
Start/Finish	Portinfer
Refreshments	Tearoom/bistro at Portinfer, café at Plémont, with pubs and cafés around La Grève de Lecq.
Transport	Bus 8 serves Portinfer, while 7b and 8 serve Plémont in summer. Bus 9 and the Red Explorer serve La Grève de Lecq, along with 7b in summer.

A fine stretch of cliff path runs between Plémont and La Grève de Lecq, and both places are accessible by bus. Moving inland, a series of quiet roads can be linked to lead back to Plémont, taking in quaint little farming settlements, fine houses and the tiny village of Portinfer. The Old Barracks at La Grève de Lecq have been developed as a visitor centre, serving as an interpretation centre for the natural wonders of the north coast.

Portinfer is a small village on a crossroads, and the Route de Plémont runs through potato fields to reach a car park and bus stop (summer only) near cliffs at **Plémont**. Signs invite you down to a beach café and a wonderful beach, but if you go down there you must climb back afterwards. Leave the car park by following a path parallel to a narrow road, continuing to a small, stone lookout tower. A path runs downhill from here, allowing the headland of **La Tête de Plémont** to be explored, as well as a concrete bunker. There are fine views of the cliffs, with the jagged Paternosters prominent out to sea. However, steps must be retraced back up to the lookout tower afterwards to continue. ◄

A derelict holiday village may be replaced by a smaller housing development on the cliff-top.

A glimpse of the beach at Plémont, which can be reached by going down steps from a café

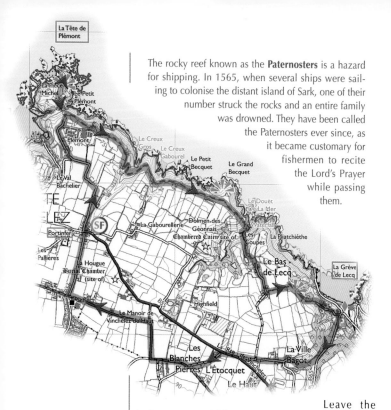

The rocky reef known as the **Paternosters** is a hazard for shipping. In 1565, when several ships were sailing to colonise the distant island of Sark, one of their number struck the rocks and an entire family was drowned. They have been called the Paternosters ever since, as it became customary for fishermen to recite the Lord's Prayer while passing them.

Fulmar, razorbill, shag, puffin and a variety of gulls can be spotted.

Leave the lookout tower and follow steps downhill and uphill at the start of the cliff path. A stone records the construction of the path in 1981, and zigzags lead down into a valley overlooking the cleft of **Le Creux Gros**. Climb round a headland and descend into another valley overlooking **Le Creux Gabourel**. After a long flight of steps uphill, an easier path continues. There is an option to take a narrow path down to the rocky outcrop of **Le Grand Becquet**, where fine views stretch back along the coast. ◄ Climb back up to the main path to continue.

A deep valley is crossed at **Les Coupes** using a long flight of steps, with an ascent into a patch of woodland at the head of the valley. Turn right at the top and follow the access road away from Lecq Clay Target Club. Turn left at

View of the beach on the way down to the little village of La Grève de Lecq

a junction at **Le Bas de Lecq** to follow a track and path more and more steeply downhill with views across the bay at **La Grève de Lecq**. ▶

To continue walking round the coast of Jersey, follow the narrow road up past the Old Barracks, referring to Walk 9.

LA GRÈVE DE LECQ

There are several points of interest around the village, as well as accommodation, pubs, cafés, restaurants, toilets and buses. Part of the watermill, Le Moulin de Lecq, dates from the 12th century and corn was ground as late as 1929. The huge millwheel is attached to shafts and cogs running through the inn. The prominent Jersey Tower standing in the middle of a car park in the village dates from 1780, and has been painted as a navigational aid.

THE OLD BARRACKS

The Old Barracks, built in 1810, stand prominently above the village. The National Trust for Jersey has restored the buildings. Further fortifications were added during the German Occupation, with concrete bunkers flanking the bay, and two searchlights powered by electricity generated at the old mill. (For more information see the start of Walk 9.)

When explorations around **La Grève de Lecq** are complete, follow the road uphill from the Prince of Wales, climbing into a wooded valley. Turn right along a concrete road. Follow this steeply uphill between densely vegetated banks to reach some fine old buildings in a huddle at **La Ville Bagot**. Turn left along a narrow tarmac road, marked as cycleway Route 1, then bear right to continue. The road is called La Petite Rue and it joins the main road for Portinfer.

Turn right as if intending to follow it in that direction, but switch to a network of quieter roads by turning left at a bus stop. Next, turn right along Rue de L'Étocquet, and right again at Les Doubles Chasses. A left turn along Rue du Nord leads through more potato fields, passing La Ferme. When **St George's Church** is reached, turn right to follow Rue de la Porte straight back to the crossroads at **Portinfer**.

WALK 9

La Grève de Lecq and Devil's Hole

Distance	12km (7½ miles)
Terrain	Easy cliff paths, with some diversions away from the coast, followed by road walking and woodland paths.
Start/Finish	La Grève de Lecq
Refreshments	Several places around La Grève de Lecq. Pub restaurants are available at La Falaise and St Mary's. Restaurant at La Mare Wine Estate.
Transport	Bus 9 and the Red Explorer serve La Grève de Lecq, along with 7b in summer. Bus 7 and the Yellow Explorer serve La Falaise, La Mare Wine Estate and St Mary's.

A fine stretch of cliff path runs between La Grève de Lecq and the Devil's Hole, though there are also notable diversions from the cliffs. A circular walk can be enjoyed by moving inland from La Falaise, taking in a couple of attractions along the way. One is a short vineyard walk, with the chance to indulge in a little wine tasting at La Mare Wine Estate. After visiting St Mary's Parish Church a lovely valley walk leads back to La Grève de Lecq.

LA GRÈVE DE LECQ

Neolithic people are known to have used the sheltered harbour at La Grève de Lecq. An Iron Age hill fort known as Le Câtel de Lecq overlooks the valley and was used until 1406. The prominent Jersey Tower standing in the middle of a car park dates from 1780, and has been painted as a navigational aid. An old guardhouse overlooking the bay, called Le Câtel Fort, was rebuilt and modified during the 1780s. The Old Barracks were built in 1810 and were restored by the National Trust for Jersey. (For more information see Walk 8.)

Leave **La Grève de Lecq** by following a narrow road, Le Chemin du Câtel, up past the Old Barracks. A grassy path on the left, flanked by bushes, leads to Le Câtel Fort, an

The Old Barracks at La Grève de Lecq serve as a visitor centre and offer basic accommodation

Basic accommodation can be arranged at the old guardhouse.

old guardhouse overlooking the bay. ◄ Continue up the road, passing potato fields, then plenty of notices warn of the Crabbé Rifle Range on the seaward side, barring access to the cliffs for a while. The hump of a hill to the left is the top of the Iron Age hill fort of Le Câtel de Lecq, with steps to the top, while to the right is the wooded valley of **Les Vaux de Lecq**. The road levels out at the Jersey Pistol Club, then there is a left turn, signposted 'cliff path', passing **Crabbé Farm**.

Beyond the farm buildings a track turns right and left, and then runs towards the cliffs; walkers should keep to the left of a parallel bridlepath route. Enjoy the fine views from the cliff top then turn right along the cliff path. Pass around Le Pré de Crabbé and note the rugged sea-stack called **L'Île Agois**.

The cliff-bound sea-stack of **L'Île Agois** features a long history of habitation, suggesting that in earlier times it was actually linked to the rest of Jersey by a rock bridge. Hut circles have been excavated, and finds have included an axe head, an arrow head, a large urn and a

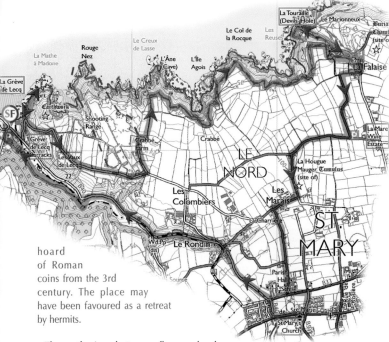

hoard
of Roman
coins from the 3rd
century. The place may
have been favoured as a retreat
by hermits.

The path rises between flowery banks
with a view of the topmost point of the stack. Turn
right and follow the path, which runs beneath a canopy
of bushes, emerging with a fine view from **Le Col de la
Rocque**. ▶ Look across the bay to spot the Devil's Hole
and the path spiralling down to it. Follow the path around
the head of the bay and make a left turn around a small
pool. Numerous cliff path and footpath signs steer the
route through fields, passing above a house in a wooded
valley. Follow a track away from the house then turn left
to follow a short wooded path to the Priory Inn at **La
Falaise**. Food and drink are available, as well as the Old
Priory Studio and a bus stop.

A narrow tarmac road runs seawards from the Priory
Inn, signposted for the Devil's Hole. The tarmac narrows
as the route drops into a wooded valley, passing a house.
Descend steps through a bracken-filled valley to reach
a viewing platform at the top of the **Devil's Hole**. ▶ The

Note the sheer rock
wall at the head
of the next rugged
bay, which is not
really seen at closer
quarters.

A ship's figurehead
was once washed
up here. It was
modified with horns
and erected as an
attraction – hence
the 'Devil's Hole'.
Formerly the pit was
called Le Creux de
Vis.

79

path swings round to a lower viewing platform allowing the very bottom of the hole to be seen. At high tide the sea might be slopping around over huge boulders at the bottom of the pit. There are fine views along the cliffs too, taking in a series of caves which are not seen from the higher cliff path, as well as views towards Sark, Guernsey and Alderney. Retrace your steps back up to the Priory Inn. ◀

To continue walking round the coast of Jersey, refer to Walk 10.

The route now heads inland, following the road between the inn and the studio. Turn right and right again to follow the 'green lane' called La Rue du Camp Durrell. Turn left through potato fields, then the next left turn leads to the entrance of **La Mare Wine Estate**.

LA MARE WINE ESTATE

La Mare was rescued from dereliction in 1968 and completely restored by the Blaney family, long-established wine merchants. They established the first commercial vineyard in the Channel Islands in 1972. The first good vintage was produced in 1976 and Queen Elizabeth II was supplied with wine on a visit to Jersey in 1978. The business expanded with a distillery producing apple brandy, while a kitchen was established to produce a range of preserves, mustards, chocolates and biscuits. 'Black Butter', a traditional spiced Jersey apple-cider preserve, is one of the most intriguing products in the range. All these products can also be obtained from the Estate's shop on King Street in St Helier. The Blaneys sold La Mare in 1997.

The shop and part of the grounds can be visited for free, but there is an entry charge for the full tour, which naturally includes opportunities to taste the wines and foodstuffs. There are rows of vines and orchards, a Vineyard Trail, wooded areas and a few animals, as well as a kitchen herb garden. There is a restaurant on site and luxury picnic baskets can be pre-ordered, enabling visitors to picnic in style in the grounds. Open daily Easter to October, tel. 01534 481178, www.lamarewineestate.com.

Leave La Mare and double back along the road, which is a 'green lane', continuing straight ahead and gently uphill along La Rue de la Hougue Mauger. Reach a huddle of houses on a hilltop and turn left down a narrower road. Turn right at the bottom along La Rue du

St Mary's Parish Church was originally known as St Mary of the Burnt Monastery

Point, then left gently uphill to the end of the 'green lane' to reach a busy road beside a school. Turn left along the busy road, then right to follow La Rue de l'Église, passing St Mary's Country Inn to reach **St Mary's Church**.

> Curiously, the old name for **St Mary's Parish Church** was St Mary of the Burnt Monastery, but there are no records of a monastery in the area, let alone one being burnt. The oldest parts of the church date from the 12th century and an exploration of the place proves to be quite interesting.

Either visit the church or turn right along the main road to pass below it. Another right turn is signposted for La Grève de Lecq, then bear left at the next junction to follow La Rue du Rondin. This road leads down to a lovely little settlement of fine buildings. Follow Le Mont de Ste Marie past a duckpond, and notice how the valley side to the right has been landscaped into an enormous garden below **Les Colombiers**. Further down the valley, there are wooded slopes to the left and very steep potato fields to the right.

After turning round a pronounced wooded bend, watch for a clear path on the left. Follow it into the woods, crossing a stream and bearing right. A fine woodland path can be followed towards the mouth of the valley. It bends to the left towards the end and joins a road. All that remains is to turn right and walk down the road into **La Grève de Lecq**.

WALK 10
La Falaise and St John

Distance	10km (6¼ miles)
Terrain	Cliff paths, followed by a mixture of busy roads and quiet 'green lanes'.
Start/Finish	The Priory Inn, La Falaise
Refreshments	The Priory Inn is at the start and finish. A pub restaurant is available at Les Fontaines. Pubs and cafés are available at St John's.
Transport	Bus 7 and the Yellow Explorer serve La Falaise. Bus 5 and the Yellow Explorer serve St John's.

Ronez, the most northerly point on Jersey, is unfortunately part of an enormous quarry and is out of bounds to walkers. However, there is a good stretch of coastal path from La Falaise to the quarry. La Route du Nord is a coastal road that can be followed from Ronez to St John's, where an interesting network of 'green lanes' and other quiet roads can be pressed into service to lead walkers in a complete circuit. One of these lanes is an old *perquage* or sanctuary path. Some fine old buildings, lovely countryside and prehistoric remains can be observed along the way.

Leave the Priory Inn at **La Falaise** by climbing a flight of steps between it and the bus stop. Turn left along a road and left again to follow a path out onto a headland. Turn right along the cliff path and there is a view of a pierced headland on the descent into **La Vallée des Mouriers**. Cross a stream at the bottom and zigzag up a path on the far side of the valley to continue along the cliffs. A view back into the valley reveals a small reservoir. The cliff path passes a block of granite announcing that this is National Trust for Jersey land.

The path climbs flights of steps over a rugged hump of gorse and granite. There is a dip in the path, then a rise through bushes that completely envelop the path. When a

The Devil's Hole is a popular visitor attraction reached from the bus stop at the Priory Inn at La Falaise. Anyone who has not already visited it should do so before leaving. See Walk 9 for details.

road and car park are reached, it is worth turning left down to a white-painted lighthouse at **Sorel**, but steps have to be retraced afterwards. There is a view of a huge quarry chewing into the cliffs at **Ronez**, the most northerly point in Jersey, but there are no paths in that direction. Walk inland along the road from Sorel, turning left at a junction to follow a busier road uphill. There is a good footway beside the road, passing the road entrance to the quarry.

RONEZ QUARRY

Ronez is usually described a 'granite' quarry, although granite is only one type of rock present. Most of the rock being quarried is diorite. There are also intermediate granodiorites and, rather unusually, gabbro too. The relationship between these igneous rock types is complex. In some places rocks of different types merge gradually into each other, while in other places they form quite separate bands. Even more unusual are granitic pipes which run through the diorite. During the German Occupation a mineral line was laid all the way through Jersey to exploit this site. The quarry has its own flag and a website, www.aggregate.com/Our-businesses/Ronez.

Ronez, the northernmost point of Jersey, is part of a huge quarry site and cannot be approached

It is a short optional extension taking only a few minutes. Sometimes the loop is closed and used as a go-kart track.

A crossroads is reached where Les Fontaines Tavern offers food and drink on the right, while the road on the left makes a loop offering a reasonable view along the cliffs from **Le Moutré**, returning to the crossroads. ◀ The main road is called **La Route du Nord** and from it wooded slopes fall down to the sea.

This stretch of coastal road, **La Route du Nord**, was built by over 2000 islanders during the German Occupation.

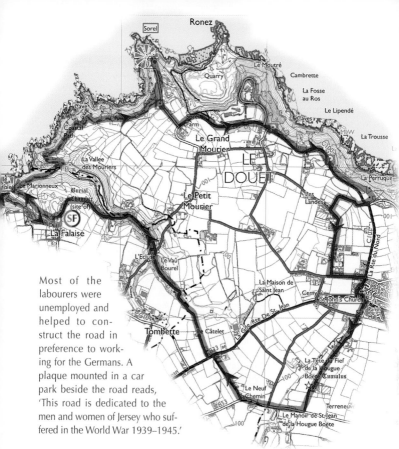

Most of the labourers were unemployed and helped to construct the road in preference to working for the Germans. A plaque mounted in a car park beside the road reads, 'This road is dedicated to the men and women of Jersey who suffered in the World War 1939–1945.'

Keep following the road, passing another car park and viewpoint. Watch for a path heading left from the road, wandering through a grassy space, returning to the road later near a junction and a stone memorial cross. ▶ From the junction, follow the least of the roads in view, the narrow 'green lane' of Rue de la Perruque. Keep turning left at other road junctions, passing a few houses until the main road is joined again. Turn right to walk straight to St John's village, reaching **St John's Parish Church**. There are a few shops nearby, as well as St John's Inn.

To continue walking round the coast of Jersey, follow the road onwards and refer to Walk 10.

ST JOHN'S PARISH CHURCH

Also known as St John in the Oaks, this is an interesting church separated from other buildings in the village by fine green spaces. The structure has grown over about 800 years from a simple chapel to a large church. Rather oddly, a pillar supporting two arches was removed so that the parishioners could get a better view during services, despite concerns that the roof might collapse! The church has eight inscribed bells, some fine stained glass and a display of ecclesiastical vessels. Outside, La Rue des Buttes is the former *perquage*, or sanctuary path, which would have been used by any criminal being banished from Jersey, provided that they reached sanctuary at the church before being caught.

St John in the Oaks, where parishioners removed a supporting arch simply to get a better view!

Leave the church by walking away from the main entrance, crossing a busy road and following a 'green lane' called La Rue des Buttes, to the right of the Salle Paroissiale. Pass St John's School and continue along a narrow road flanked by an avenue of horse chestnuts. Walk past the large house called Les Buttes and other fine houses. Note the wooded hump to the right of the road, which is a tumulus with the splendid name of **La Tête du Fief de la Hougue Boëte**, opposite houses at Greenfields.

Turn right at the end of the lane and follow another road, **Le Neuf Chemin**, past a junction where 'School Bus' is painted on the road. Turn right at Le Mottée, which is signposted as a 'green lane' called La Rue du Muet, and 'no entry'. At the end of the road, a quick left and right turn lead across the main road and onto another 'green lane', La Rue d'Enfer. This narrow road passes through fields, then descends through a lovely wooded valley called **Le Vaû Bourel**. The road twists through a huddle of houses then continues down to a crossroads. Go straight through the crossroads to follow Le Chemin des Hougues downhill. Later the road rises and leads out of the valley and back to the Priory Inn at **La Falaise**.

Alternative Option

There is an option, just as the road rises, to turn right down a track into **La Vallée des Mouriers**. The track passes a small reservoir and joins the coastal path that was followed earlier in the day. Turn left uphill, onto a headland, and turn left inland to re-join the road near the Priory Inn.

WALK 11
Bonne Nuit Bay and St John

Distance	8km (5 miles)
Terrain	Some of the cliffs paths are quite steep and feature flights of steps. The roads running inland are fairly quiet, but occasionally busy.
Start/Finish	St John's Parish Church
Refreshments	Pub and café at St John's. Beach café at Bonne Nuit Bay. A snacks van may be available at Les Platons. A shop is passed at Les Hautes Croix.
Transport	Bus 5 serves St John's and Les Hautes Croix. Bus 4 serves Bonne Nuit Bay and Les Platons. The Yellow Explorer serves St John's, Les Platons and Les Hautes Croix.

A fine cliff path lies north of St John's, leading to Bonne Nuit Bay, where a variety of paths offers options to walk at a high or low level. Spend a while exploring Bonne Nuit Bay, with particular attention to the circuit offered by La Vallette Walk. Views are remarkably varied if each and every path can be included. A route using fairly quiet roads, with a busy interlude, can be used to return inland to St John's, following La Rue Militaire.

St John's village boasts a fine green space around its parish church, St John in the Oaks (see Walk 10 for information). Find a crescent of small shops behind the church, and walk between the Spar shop and a chemist, along La Rue du Temple. Bear slightly right at a junction, walk past houses old and new and turn left along La Rue de la Ville Guyon. Ville Guyon is a large house on the right of this road. Turn left at **La Cocagne**, at the end of the road, following La Route du Nord downhill. Turn right along a narrow road and track signposted 'cliff path', not the track to La Saline granite and marble works. Another 'cliff path' sign indicates a narrow path flanked by gorse, followed by a flight of steps up a

slope of bracken and heather beneath the tall **Frémont Transmitting Station**.

Down at the foot of the cliffs, the **Wolf's Caves** were once a notable attraction, but they are no longer safe to approach. The overgrown steps seen on the slope used to lead into a rocky cleft full of large boulders, where little caves could be visited at low water.

Pass a large building, formerly a restaurant, and continue along the cliff path. The rocky headland of **La Tête de Frémont** suddenly reveals superb views over Bonne Nuit Bay and its little pier. Spend a while studying the layout of paths around the bay, which will help when making choices later. ▶ Descend a steep and winding flight of steps, reaching a road at the bottom. Turn left down the road to **Bonne Nuit Bay**, then at a junction, either turn left to visit the pier and its café, or turn right to continue the walk.

Apple trees in bloom inland from Les Platons, once a common sight when cider was produced

La Vallette Walk is a circuit on the steep slope rising from the bay, while further ahead, high and low-level paths can be spotted.

89

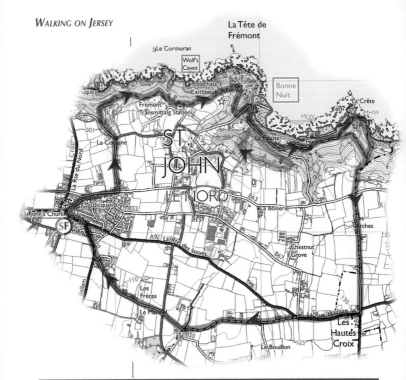

BONNE NUIT BAY

There is a touching little tale accounting for the name 'Bonne Nuit'. It is said that Charles II left Jersey from this bay, before the island finally came under Cromwellian control at the end of the Civil War. He is reputed to have said *'Bonne nuit, belle Jersey'*. Doubt is cast on the tale because the place-name of *Bono Nocte* was first recorded in the 12th century, and appears to owe its origin to a medieval chapel. Curiously, before that time the name was quite the opposite: *Mala Nocte*!

The road climbing from Bonne Nuit Bay is signposted for Bouley Bay and passes a bus stop. Just across the road is a National Trust for Jersey sign indicating La Vallette Walk.

La Vallette Walk

This short circular walk is confined to a rugged slope, and if followed, the path leads back to the road again. The loop is therefore an optional extra, but also highly recommended, since it offers fine views over the bay. Follow the path uphill to the left, rising across a bracken slope sparsely planted with trees, becoming rockier towards the top. Turn right and enjoy a fine panorama as the path runs past a couple of rocky outcrops. The descent zigzags through an ivy-floored woodland, ending on a slope of bracken and gorse to return to the road. The extra distance is around 1km (½ mile).

Follow the road uphill then turn left down a narrow road for the **Cheval Roc Hotel**, which is also signposted for Bouley Bay. A track runs to the right of the hotel, reaching a stone block indicating the 'Upper Path' and the 'Lower Path'. Either may be followed, but if using the 'Upper Path', then start climbing immediately, and later turn right to keep climbing. The track, meanwhile, runs down to **La Crête**.

The building at **La Crête**, dating from 1830, is the only one remaining from fortifications constructed

Dating from 1830, the stone guardhouse at La Crête offers an unusual accommodation base

at various times around Bonne Nuit Bay, though the bay was never approached by any invasion force. This stout stone guardhouse, with its distinctive conical stone roof, is available as holiday accommodation through Jersey Heritage, **www.jerseyheritage.org/ heritage-holiday-lets**.

To continue walking round the coast of Jersey, refer to Walk 12, and bear in mind that either the 'Lower Path' or 'Upper Path' could be used.

The 'Lower Path' wanders round a rugged bay, reaching a junction. Turn right and climb steps, passing a point where the 'Upper Path' joins. Climb further flights of steps to reach a car park at Les Platons, where there might be a snacks van. There are also bus services on the road, La Rue des Platons. ◄

Follow a road inland from a junction, signposted for St Helier and called La Rue du Bechet ès Cats. The road passes fine buildings at **Les Arches**, then reaches a grocery shop at a staggered crossroads at **Les Hautes Croix**. Turn right as signposted for St John, following the busy road, **La Rue Militaire**. The busy road later swings right, so keep left down a quieter road, which is still La Rue Militaire, passing Le Claire Stables. Turn right at a junction at Ashley Court and pass Chapelle des Frères, which is the Boys' Brigade Island Headquarters at **Les Frères**. ◄

There are some fine houses along the road.

At the end of Les Chenolles, turn right onto a busier road, then left into **St John's**, to finish back at the parish church.

WALK 12
La Belle Hougue and Trinity

Distance	10km (6¼ miles)
Terrain	Some cliff paths can be steep, with plenty of steps. Roads used inland are mostly quiet, but occasionally busy.
Start/Finish	Les Platons
Refreshments	A snacks van might be available at Les Platons. Beach café and hotel bar at Bouley Bay. A pub is available near Trinity Church.
Transport	Bus 4 and the Yellow Explorer link Les Platons with the top of Bouley Hill and Trinity. Buses also serve Bouley Bay in summer.

The walk around La Belle Hougue to Bouley Bay is a varied and beautiful coastal walk. There are fine, flower-fringed cliff paths, with areas of trees and bushes on some of the rugged slopes. The highest ground in Jersey is in this area, not that anyone visits Jersey to climb hills! At the end of the coastal walk a famous road with hairpin bends is climbed on Bouley Hill, and roads lead inland to the lovely Holy Trinity Church. More quiet roads are linked to return to the starting point at Les Platons.

Start at the car park at **Les Platons**, high above Bonne Nuit Bay and **Le Havre Giffard**. Face the sea and turn right to follow a path, known as the 'Upper Path', away from the car park, signposted for Bouley Bay. ▶ The path runs gradually downhill and turns around a little valley, beneath the whirling radar dish of an Aeronautical Receiver Station. The path drops and climbs across the slope, and it is important to keep left, downhill, at a junction, and not follow a path uphill and inland. Turn round another little valley and climb across a slope of bushes, reaching a junction with the 'Lower Path' at a marker stone. ▶

Continue round a rugged headland called **La Belle Hougue**, often covered in bushes but offering fine views

There is also a 'Lower Path' on the rugged slopes, as described in Walk 11.

Anyone who walks both the 'Upper Path' and 'Lower Path' will probably agree that the lower one is the tougher.

Looking back to Bonne Nuit Bay and La Tête de Frémont from La Belle Hougue

Note the monument to British and French Commandos who took part in 'Operation Hardtack 28' during Christmas of 1943.

along the cliffs. Follow the path onwards and down steps in sweeping zigzags towards the sea, ending with a right turn. The grassy path bottoms out then climbs uphill flanked by flowers and bracken. It continues in a switchback fashion and leads down to **Le Petit Port**, where a cottage called the Wolf's Lair stands in a patch of woodland. ◀

Follow a wooded track up through a valley and turn left at a marker stone at a junction. There are no views as a well-worn path winds up a densely-wooded slope. Keep to the left and the path emerges onto an open headland again, though there are still quite a number of trees and bushes along the way, followed by banks of bracken and gorse. There is one brief view of the harbour wall at Bouley Bay, easily missed, before the path drops inland. Go down steps and turn left along a grassy track above a potato field.

The track promises a gradual descent, but in fact there is a steep and rugged slope ahead, where the path twists and turns down flights of steps to reach the road near the Undercliff Guest House. Turning left leads down to **The Water's Edge Hotel**, bar, café, harbour and toilets. If none of these is needed, turn right and walk up the road. ◀

To continue walking round the coast of Jersey, go behind the Water's Edge Hotel and refer to Walk 13.

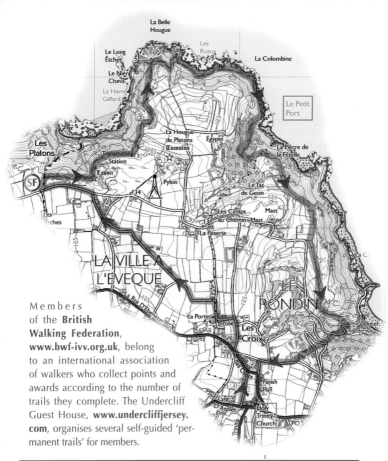

Members of the **British Walking Federation**, **www.bwf-ivv.org.uk**, belong to an international association of walkers who collect points and awards according to the number of trails they complete. The Undercliff Guest House, **www.undercliffjersey.com**, organises several self-guided 'permanent trails' for members.

BOULEY BAY

A large harbour development was planned for this deep-water bay in the 19th century, but access inland was difficult because of the steep slopes, so the scheme was shelved. For a time, Bouley Bay was a noted smugglers' haunt, and it may well have been the smugglers who started telling tales of 'Le Tchan du Bouôlé'. This was supposed to be a huge black dog with eyes the size of saucers, that wandered round the woods and cliffs of Bouley Bay, especially during storms.

*Dropping steeply
downhill to the
Water's Edge Hotel at
Bouley Bay*

Follow the road uphill and inland. After passing the Undercliff Guest House, it is possible to short-cut the hairpin bends by following a woodland path steeply uphill. Every time the road is encountered, cross over and continue up flights of steps, eventually reaching a car park at the top of the hill at Le Parc de la Petite Falaise.

Bouley Bay Hill Climb is a motor vehicle time trial held on the tight hairpin bends of Bouley Hill, and when it takes place the road is closed to all other traffic, including bus services and walkers! The first event was held in 1920 and the only significant break was during the German Occupation. The organisers are the Jersey Motorcycle and Light Car Club, **www.jerseymotorsport. com**. The culmination of these trials is the British Hill Climb Championship each July.

Turn right to follow the road away from the car park, turning left to follow Rue du Presbytère to Holy Trinity Parish Church. Follow a path through the churchyard, rather than the road around it. The Trinity Arms lies left of the church, along the main road. Take a break to explore the church.

> Some of the oldest altar-ware on Jersey is preserved at **Holy Trinity Church**. The oldest masonry in the church is the tower and spire, parts of which date back to the 12th century. This is curious as those parts were struck three times by lightning in the 17th century! The church seems to stand isolated from other buildings, but those buildings closest to it are fine stone edifices well worth a moment of admiration.

Walk through the main gate to leave the churchyard. Turn right and right again to follow La Rue au Sellier. Turn left along busy **La Rue des Croix**, and turn right at an obelisk memorial to follow quiet La Rue du Tas de Geon. Walk gently uphill and turn left down La Rue de Cambrai, then turn right and continue gently uphill. A left turn leads onto La Rue du Nord; follow it past all junctions and straight through a crossroads. Continue along Rue de la Petite Lande, with masts and a whirling radar dish off to the right. A left turn at the next junction leads back along La Rue des Platons to reach the car park at **Les Platons** where the walk started.

WALK 13
Bouley Bay and Rozel

Distance	10km (6¼ miles)
Terrain	Cliff paths, with some steep stretches up and down, followed by quiet and busy roads.
Start/Finish	Bouley Bay
Refreshments	Beach café and hotel bar at Bouley Bay. Restaurants and cafés at Rozel. Restaurant available at Durrell Wildlife Conservation Trust.
Transport	Bus 4 and the Yellow Explorer serve Bouley Bay in summer. Bus 3 and the Green Explorer serve Rozel. Buses 3a, 3b, 23 and the Green and Yellow Explorers serve the Durrell Wildlife Conservation Trust.

An interesting and varied roller-coaster cliff-top path runs between Bouley Bay and Rozel. After exploring the attractive harbour area, the route heads inland along a 'green lane' through an exotically wooded valley. Busy roads are encountered on the way to the Durrell Wildlife Conservation Trust, formerly known as Jersey Zoo. Hours could easily pass while exploring this place, but if any time remains then walkers can return to Bouley Bay.

If walking outside the summer season, restructure the route to start from the Durrell Wildlife Conservation Trust.

During the summer there are buses down the hairpin road to **Bouley Bay** and the Water's Edge Hotel. ◄ Look down on the harbour to see boats sheltering behind a stout stone wall. Follow the road inland and turn left to climb a flight of steps between the Water's Edge Hotel and Undercliff Guest House. Turn left along a woodland path, passing junctions with other paths to continue along the coast. The path runs along a low cliff-line overlooking the small rocky island of **L'Islet**. Climb a flight of steps, then continue along a roller-coaster path, with fine views back to Bouley Bay. Follow the path downhill a short way, then uphill and through a wooded valley. ◄ Walk behind a cliff-top cottage called Son de la Mer.

The main road is never far inland, and there are a few access points marked leading to it.

La Tête des Hougues is a rugged, flowery headland with fine cliff views in both directions. A fort can be seen ahead, perched on the cliff edge at **L'Étacquerel**. It can be reached by a short path, but cannot be entered.

Looking back across Bouley Bay from the coast path near the tiny isle of L'Islet

> **L'Étacquerel Fort** was built in 1836, and on the approach path a bridge spans a dry moat. The building has been restored and is now let as basic accommodation for large groups by Jersey Heritage, **www.jerseyheritage.org/heritage-holiday-lets**. Defensive structures were built around Bouley Bay over the years, but none was deemed particularly effective.

The path zigzags down into a little wooded valley, turns round a little point and is flanked by bushes. There are a couple of conglomerate rock steps along the way, while a prominent building above the cliff path used to be a hotel. Climb up a wooded slope and walk beside some potato fields for a while. There is an exit onto the main road if required, before the path runs through bushes and turns around an attractive little bay.

99

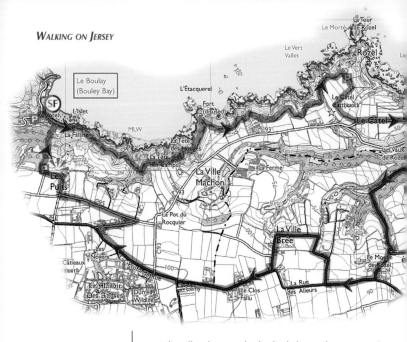

A visit is optional, as steps have to be retraced afterwards to a car park.

A headland is reached which has a fine view of the white-painted White Rock, a navigational aid also known as **La Tour de Rozel**. The rock is not quite an island, but only a narrow neck of rock links it to the rest of Jersey. ◄ Note also the impressive house called Fort Rozel which is on the next headland, though there is no access along the coast in that direction.

Although not immediately apparent, **Le Câtel de Rozel** is a stout Iron Age earthwork built to enclose the headland to form a promontory fort that could easily be defended. Four large hoards of coins found on this site have been dated from around 60 to 50BC.

Follow a track inland from the car park, through the fields, and turn left when buildings are reached. The road later descends as the Rue du Câtel, which bends to the right and overlooks the harbour at **Rozel**. Turn left at the bottom, where there is a restaurant, and walk along La

Le Nez du Guet

Le Havre de Rozel

Brecque du Nord to reach the delightful little harbour. There are plenty of places to eat and drink, as well as toilets.

Turn round and walk back along La Brecque du Nord, turn left and follow the road until a right turn can be made at The Rozel bar and restaurant. ▶ There is a bus stop just beyond The Rozel. Follow the road, which is a 'green lane', up though La Vallée de Rozel, passing through exotic woodlands around Château Le Chaire Hotel. ▶ Turn left later to continue more steeply uphill, then keep straight ahead at a junction, along Rue du Moulin. Look carefully to the right to see the stone tower of a former windmill, **Le Moulin de Rozel**, beside a house. The old tower, dating from the 16th century, was used as an observation post during the German Occupation.

Turn right at the end of the road, following a road that can be quite busy at times. The only option for avoiding the traffic is to turn right along the 'green lane' called Rue des Muriaux, then keep turning left through **La Ville Brée**

To continue walking round the coast of Jersey, keep left before The Rozel and refer to Walk 14.

From 1851 the chateau's grounds were developed by the Victorian horticulturalist, Samuel Curtis.

The colourful Rozel Harbour is worth visiting and there are places offering food and drink

until the main road is joined again. Turn right at the end of Rue de la Ville Brée, following signs for Durrell Wildlife at the next busy main road junction.

DURRELL WILDLIFE CONSERVATION TRUST

This was formerly known as Jersey Zoo, founded by the late Gerald Durrell in the grounds of Les Augrès Manor in 1963. Note the 'dodo' gateposts as you enter. The Trust was established specifically for conservation of endangered species, to prevent them becoming 'as dead as a dodo'. The grounds are hilly and well watered, with wooded areas and a variety of habitats. Visitors may wander round just to look at the animals, but subtly-worded messages preach conservation at every opportunity. The lowland gorillas are very popular, and a children's climbing area lies beside a climbing area used by orang-utans! There are several varieties of New World monkeys as well as lemurs, bats, reptiles and birds. A maze of paths leads through the different habitats, and there is also an orchard and organic farm.

Keepers give regular talks and are on hand to answer any questions that visitors might pose. There is a visitor centre, bookshop, gift shop and a restaurant on site. The grounds offer an interesting botanical tour and the stone buildings of Les Augrès are to be admired. Next door at Les Noyers, students from around the world attend courses which are specific to their needs, whether they have responsibility for managing wildlife in an entire country, or simply care for a small part of a zoo.

An important captive breeding and release scheme is in operation, networking with zoos and reserves worldwide. On a more local scale, choughs have been bred and released onto the cliffs of Jersey, after a century of absence. Visitors are invited to support the work of the Durrell Wildlife Conservation Trust. There is an entry charge, tel. 01534 860000, www.durrell.org.

The French invaded Jersey by way of Bouley Bay in 1549, but were heavily defeated in this area.

Leaving the entrance, walk further along the main road, La Rue Profonde, and turn sharp right as signposted for Rozel Harbour along Rue du Becquet. A sharp left turn along Rue des Bouillons follows. When a crossroads is reached at **Les Puits**, turn right to walk along Rue de la Falaise, turning left to reach a car park at Jardin d'Olivet. The '*jardin*' is a rugged common of gorse scrub above Bouley Bay. ◀

Walk to the bottom corner of the car park and exit left to follow a path steeply down through woodland. Turn left halfway down, after passing a curious folly, and cut across the wooded slope. Turn right at a hairpin bend, following the path down to a junction at the bottom of the slope. Go down steps used earlier in the day, between the Undercliff Guest House and Water's Edge Hotel on the way back to the harbour at **Bouley Bay**.

Sandy, fertile soil is ploughed and planted with Jersey Royal potatoes near La Ville Brée

WALK 14
Rozel and St Catherine's

Distance	11km (7 miles)
Terrain	Easy walking on paths, tracks and roads. Some of the woodland paths can be muddy.
Start/Finish	Rozel Harbour
Refreshments	Plenty of choice around Rozel. Café available at St Catherine's Breakwater and a pub at St Martin's.
Transport	Bus 3 and the Green Explorer serve Rozel and St Martin's. Bus 1b serves St Catherine's Breakwater and St Catherine's Tower. Buses 3a and 23 also serve St Martin's.

The coastal walk between Rozel and St Catherine's is not always on the coast. There are diversions inland at a couple of points, using roads rather than paths, but there is plenty of interest along the way, and views of the distant rocks of Les Écréhous. The massive St Catherine's Breakwater provides a popular walk in its own right, sheltering St Catherine's Bay. Strange to think it was intended to shelter a naval base! Moving inland, St Catherine's Woods are rich in trees, flowers and ferns, providing a lovely walk up to St Martin's Church. Quiet 'green lanes' and wooded valleys offer a route back to Rozel.

Start at **Rozel** after having a look round the village and harbour. Walk up the road from the harbour, La Brecque du Nord, turning left at the top and keeping left at The Rozel bar and restaurant. The road climbs and features good views over the harbour. Turn sharp left along a track signposted 'Public Footpath to Le Scez', and follow it down into a wooded valley, zigzagging towards the bottom and passing a little pool. Climb over a wooded rise, then look to the left to spot an old guardhouse and the **Dolmen du Couperon**.

Le Dolmen du Couperon is a Late Neolithic gallery grave dating from 3250–2850BC, which has been

Looking back to Rozel Harbour and its breakwater

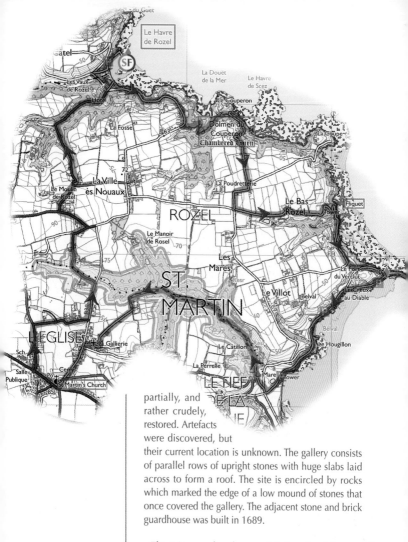

partially, and
rather crudely,
restored. Artefacts
were discovered, but
their current location is unknown. The gallery consists
of parallel rows of upright stones with huge slabs laid
across to form a roof. The site is encircled by rocks
which marked the edge of a low mound of stones that
once covered the gallery. The adjacent stone and brick
guardhouse was built in 1689.

There is a road-end car park below the dolmen and
guardhouse. Follow the narrow road away from the car
park, zigzagging up a wooded slope, a National Trust for
Jersey property called Le Grand Côtil de la Côte Pallot.

St Catherine's Breakwater stretches out to sea and offers an optional there-and-back extension

Continue through fields on top, turning right and left before reaching a crossroads at the end of Rue de Scez. Turn left to follow Rue de la Perruque, which is signposted for Fliquet Bay. The road runs downhill and zigzags past an old fortified building (a folly restored as a dwelling), and passes the **Fliquet Tower** above a beach. Follow the road uphill past Fliquet House before turning left along a path across a wooded slope. Another left turn follows a well-worn path down to another road. Walk straight ahead to reach **St Catherine's Breakwater**, where a café and toilets are located.

ST CATHERINE'S BREAKWATER

This immense stone breakwater, and a shorter one at nearby L'Archirondel, were planned to enclose a naval base when there were fears of a French invasion. Construction took place from 1847 to 1855, but only one breakwater was completed. By all means walk to the end and back, adding 1.5km (1 mile) to the day's walk, using upper and lower walkways. A couple of concrete structures were built nearby during the German Occupation, but what cannot be seen is an elaborate tunnel system carved from the adjoining headland. The geology of the area is interesting. The conglomerate rock contains pebbles from some of Jersey's older igneous rocks, which has in turn been intruded by later igneous dykes.

Lying far offshore, the rocky islets of **Les Écréhous** are included in the parish of St Martin and are occasionally inhabited by Jersey fishermen. They were subjected to a massive invasion of French fishermen in 1994 in a dispute over fishing. The rocks are important for a variety of gulls and terns, as well as shags and cormorants, and the area has been designated as a 'Ramsar' site. A mere handful of hardy fishermen have lived on Les Écréhous for extended periods and been crowned there as 'kings'.

Follow the road onwards round the headland, passing the Jersey Canoe Club boat-house and St Catherine's Sailing Club. The headland has been extensively quarried and a tunnel system built during the German Occupation is now used as an underground fish farm. Turn left at a road junction and pick up a coastal path. This exploits a rugged slope between the road and the sea, often wooded and bushy, around St Catherine's Bay. After a rocky stretch, the head of the bay is marked by **St Catherine's Tower**, a fine Jersey Tower. ◀

To continue walking round the coast of Jersey, pass the tower and refer to Walk 15.

The route heads inland from the tower, turning left along a nearby road to reach a crossroads. Turn right along a road marked 'Access only to St Catherine's Woods', followed quickly by a left turn up a narrower road, reaching a small car park and a notice for St Catherine's Woods Nature Reserve. A path continues alongside the small **Maseline Reservoir**, which was built during the German Occupation.

ST CATHERINE'S WOODS

Around 200 species of trees and plants thrive in this damp valley, with ferns being a special feature. The understorey includes elder, medlar, hazel and snowy mespil. Rocky areas bear mosses, sea campion and English stonecrop. Squirrels in the woods were imported from England and are not native to Jersey. The little grassy strip in the valley is managed as a hay meadow. Being inaccessible to heavy machinery, it is cut and raked by hand, and as the valley floor is damp, cutting is done late when the grasses and flowers have dried and set seed. As a result the meadow features over 100 plant species, including some that are uncommon around Jersey, such as opposite-leaved golden saxifrage, fool's watercress and winged St John's wort. Insects and butterflies are important, and birds and small mammals feed in the meadow and use the surrounding woods for cover. The walk through St Catherine's Woods is based on the old *perquage* or sanctuary path from St Martin's Church to the shore.

Cross a set of stepping stones over the river beyond the head of the reservoir, then cross back over more stepping stones. The valley is steep-sided, rock-walled in places, enclosing a narrow, flowery meadow. There are a couple of interpretative notice-boards along the way. Avoid a flight of steps to the left, signed 'public footpath'. Turn right at the next path junction, then left at the one afterwards, walking uphill. ▶ The path broadens and becomes a road beside a farm. Follow the road through fields, later passing the Chapelle Wesleyenne and other buildings, reaching a busy road. Turn left up to **St Martin's Parish Church**, which is worth exploring. The Royal is a pub to the left of the church, while a shop and tea room lie to the right.

Some of these paths can be muddy after rain.

St Martin's Parish Church has had its spire demolished twice by bolts of lightning

The **parish church of St Martin Le Vieux** dates back at least to the 11th century. Originally the building had a thatched roof, and when a heavier stone roof was added the walls needed strengthening with buttresses. This was achieved at some points by using old gravestones. That was not the end of structural problems, as the church spire has twice been demolished by bolts of lightning!

Follow the road gently uphill from the shop and tea room and turn right just as the **Salle Publique de Saint Martin** is reached. The road, a 'green lane', is called Rue des Raisies and it runs straight through potato fields. Turn right down Rue de la Fosse au Gres, passing a little duck pond in a dip. Turn left down a busy road, back into St Catherine's Woods. Turn left down a 'green lane', Rue de la Pallotterie, crossing the valley to climb La Rue du Blanc Pignon. Turn left along a busy road, then right onto a 'green lane' called Rue du Moulin.

The stone tower of a former windmill, **Le Moulin de Rozel**, can be seen in the grounds of a house to the left. The tower dates from the 16th century and was used as an observation post during the German Occupation. Turn left down through La Vallée de Rozel, turning right at the bottom. Pass Château La Chaire Hotel in an exotically wooded part of the valley. ◄ The bus terminus is reached before The Rozel bar and restaurant, and any spare time can be spent exploring **Rozel**.

From 1851 the Chateau's grounds were developed by the Victorian horticulturalist, Samuel Curtis.

WALK 15
Gorey and Queen's Valley

Distance	13km (8 miles)
Terrain	Easy coastal walking, with steep slopes around Gorey, and a variety of paths and 'green lanes' inland.
Start/Finish	St Catherine's Tower
Refreshments	Café available at Archirondel. Plenty of choice around Gorey. Hotel bar available at Grouville.
Transport	Bus 1b serves St Catherine's Tower, Gorey and Grouville Station. Bus 1 also serves Gorey and Grouville Station. Bus 3a serves the head of Queen's Valley Reservoir. The Green Explorer serves Gorey, Grouville Station and the head of Queen's Valley Reservoir.

A pleasant coastal walk runs round St Catherine's Bay to Mont Orgueil Castle and Gorey. Allow plenty of time to explore this remarkable, romantically situated hill-top castle. Heading inland past Grouville Station the walk maintains its watery theme with a stroll alongside Queen's Valley Reservoir. There are good shoreline paths and the reservoir is couched in a wooded valley. A circuit can be completed by linking quiet 'green lanes', passing several fine stone houses along the way back to St Catherine's Bay.

St Catherine's (White) Tower, a Jersey Tower, dates from the 1780s, and has been painted white as a landmark. The beach alongside was a shipbuilding site in the late 19th century. The lifeboat slipway bears a late medieval cross, which was discovered only in 1990. It may once have been mounted on the gables of St Agatha's, a little church which once stood nearby, or it could be the remains of an old wayside cross.

A bus runs close to St Catherine's Tower at the head of St Catherine's Bay. Walk southwards from the tower, following a path along the top of a stout, stone sea wall. The wall

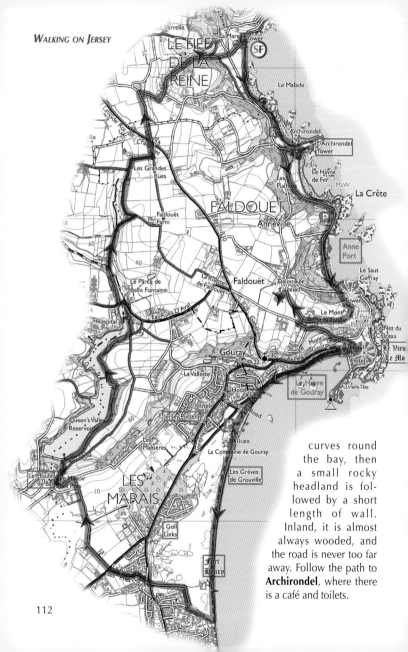

curves round the bay, then a small rocky headland is followed by a short length of wall. Inland, it is almost always wooded, and the road is never too far away. Follow the path to **Archirondel**, where there is a café and toilets.

Archirondel is named after La Roche Rondel, which bears a Jersey Tower, painted striking red and white, built in the 1790s. The tower is now let as holiday accommodation by Jersey Heritage, **www.jerseyheritage.org/heritage-holiday-lets**. The short breakwater alongside should have matched the massive St Catherine's Breakwater, built in the middle of the 19th century, but building was abandoned.

Head inland to the main coastal road and turn left. Follow the road with care, then walk on a wide, grassy verge. The road rises and turns round a fine rocky headland at **La Crête**, then descends towards **Anne Port**. Walk past toilets, a slipway and rows of houses on the way round the little bay. The road climbs, and on the way watch for a National Trust for Jersey path across the road from a timbered house. Follow the path as it zigzags above the road, climbing from woods to Victoria Tower on **Mont St Nicolas**.

This unusual Martello tower, **Victoria Tower**, was built in 1837, and was the last to be built in Jersey. It is surrounded by a dry moat spanned by a drawbridge. It was built to deny enemy forces the advantage of gaining height on Mont St Nicolas to attack nearby Mont Orgueil Castle. It is a National Trust for Jersey property and offers basic accommodation.

Follow a track away from the woods and continue along a narrow road passing some masts and houses. Turn left at a road junction, then left again along another narrow road. However, by turning right the nearby **Dolmen de Faldouët** can be visited. Simply follow the signposts.

The large Neolithic **Dolmen de Faldouët** dates from around 2500BC. A stone passage has been exposed, and originally it would have had capstones along its length and a huge mound completely covering it. The very last chamber is the only part to retain its capstone, an immense slab of rock weighing some 23 tonnes.

The Dolmen de Faldouët has a chamber covered by a capstone weighing an estimated 23 tonnes

Enjoy views of Mont Orgueil Castle while descending a road, Mont de la Garenne, marked 'no entry' and leading down to a busy road. Turn left up the main road, then right onto Castle Green for **Mont Orgueil Castle**. Spend as long as necessary exploring all the nooks and crannies of the place. Afterwards, a paved path called La P'tite Ruelle Muchie drops to **Gorey Harbour**, where there are food, drink, toilets and bus services.

MONT ORGUEIL CASTLE

The promontory bearing Mont Orgueil Castle may have been settled in the Neolithic and Iron Ages. The imposing castle dates from the 13th century and was built after King John lost Normandy to France. Construction took place over several centuries, continually upgrading the defences as the nature of warfare developed. Explorations commence in the Lower Ward, and several flights of steps and gates lead up to the Middle Ward and Upper Ward. Some rooms have been restored and contain costumed models. The French laid siege to the castle several times in the 14th century and occupied it from 1461–68. By 1593 a decision was taken to replace Mont Orgueil Castle with a new fortification in St Aubin's Bay, which became Elizabeth Castle. Apart from some late 17th century repairs, the only other military development came during the German Occupation, when some of the higher parts were made into observation towers. The castle is managed by Jersey Heritage and there is an entry charge, tel. 01534 853292, www.jerseyheritage.org. There is a café on site.

Gorey Harbour has little historical connection with Mont Orgueil Castle or nearby Gorey Village; rather, the harbour owes its development to once-prolific oyster beds. There were more oysters in the early 19th century than Jersey fishermen could manage, so they were joined by English fishermen. This was not without its problems, as new housing and other facilities needed to be built. Other oyster beds were seeded in Grouville Bay, but the fishermen could not wait for them to mature, and the Jersey Militia had to be called out to prevent overfishing, which led to arrests, riots and other disturbances. In the end, overfishing practically destroyed the industry.

Mont Orgueil Castle and Gorey Harbour could take a long time to explore properly

Follow the promenade away from the harbour, walking between the sea and the colourful swathe of Gorey Gardens. The promenade ends at the Beach Hotel. Two options can be considered, depending on the tide. If the tide is out, then the sandy beach can be followed around Grouville Bay. If the tide is in, then stay inland of the Beach Hotel, cross a grassy rise beyond, then walk along a sea wall. Note that the Royal Jersey Golf Course is alongside, so do not stray inland. **Fort Henry** is passed and a concrete promenade path is reached. ◄

To continue walking round the coast of Jersey, follow the promenade and refer to Walk 16.

The square tower of **Fort Henry** was originally known as Fort Conway and was built in 1760. It stands on the Royal Jersey Golf Course and its seaward side is flanked by two concrete bunkers built during the German Occupation. The Germans removed about one million tons of sand from Grouville Bay and used it to build defensive structures all around Jersey. A railway line was constructed to facilitate transport. The curious projections sticking out from the top of Fort Henry were added by the Germans to carry searchlights.

The well-wooded shores of Queen's Valley Reservoir are popular with walkers and fishermen

Head inland past the Royal Jersey Golf Club, reaching the main road at a bus stop at Grouville Station. ▶ Another road continues directly inland beside the Beausite Hotel. When another crossroads is reached beside a graveyard, walk straight ahead along a narrow road, La Cache des Prés, through fields. Turn left at the top, around the grounds of **Le Manoir des Prés**, and walk down to **Le Moulin de Bas**.

Note the sculpture of Harry Varden, local golfer and the first Briton to win the United States Open.

Turn right at the entrance to **Queen's Valley Reservoir**, following a road that loops round a small pond. Climb steps on the right to reach the top of the grassy reservoir dam. Do not cross the dam, but follow a wooded track onwards. A bridge later spans the reservoir, but do not cross it. ▶ The large building across the reservoir is **St Saviour's Hospital**. A car park is reached beside a small upper dam, where ducks and geese are usually present. Leave the car park and turn left along a busy road, then right along a quiet road.

Walk 18 follows a path on the other side of the reservoir. See the route description for information about the reservoir.

Follow La Rue de la Chouquetterie further up the valley, and keep right to follow a 'green lane' beyond Les Vaux Farm. The road climbs and turns sharply left to pass a house called La Chouquetterie. This next road is called Rue du Bouillon, and is followed straight past a junction, followed by a right-hand bend. Turn left along La Rue des Alleurs, passing between houses, then cross a main road at a bus stop. Continue straight ahead and turn right when a busier road is reached. This is La Mont de la Mare St Catherine, and it leads down through a crossroads to return to **St Catherine's Tower**.

WALK 16
Grouville and St Clement's

Distance	13km (8 miles)
Terrain	Some promenade paths, but also road walking or rugged beach walking between tides. Roads are used inland and some are quite busy.
Start/Finish	Grouville Station
Refreshments	Pubs at Seymour Slipway and Le Hocq. Cafés available at La Roque and Le Hocq.
Transport	Bus 1 serves the coast road. Buses 1b, 2c and the Green Explorer serve various points inland. All these buses serve Grouville Station.

Walkers who have been picking off stretches of Jersey's coastline in a clockwise circuit from St Helier will end with this stretch from Grouville Station back towards St Helier. There are some good promenade paths, but also some road walking or rugged beach walking. Coastal fortifications are very evident, and the area is very built up, with a suburban appearance. A huge amount of rocky ground is exposed at low water, with reefs and rock pools extending far into the distance. A circuit can be created by completing a road-walk inland afterwards, passing Grouville Parish Church.

JERSEY EASTERN RAILWAY

The Jersey Eastern Railway was constructed in 1873, from St Helier to Gorey. Stations and halts along the line included St Helier Snow Hill, St Helier Green Street, St Luke's, Georgetown, Grève d'Azette, Samarès, Pontorson Lane Halt, Le Hocq, Pontac, Le Bourg, La Rocque, Fauvic, Grouville and Gorey. An extension to Gorey Pier came as late as 1891. The development of bus services caused the line to suffer and it was closed in 1929. There was a brief redevelopment of the line from 1941, during the German Occupation, but the whole railway system was dismantled by 1946. There is a plan to re-open part of the old line for walkers and cyclists.

Start at Grouville Station, the 'station' being a bus stop at a crossroads near the Beausite Hotel. ▸ Follow the access road to the Royal Jersey Golf Club. **Fort Henry** can be seen towards the end of the road, but there is no direct access to it over the golf course. At the end of the road a track runs towards the sea. Turn right along a concrete promenade path on top of a sea wall, passing houses and gardens. **Jersey Tower No 5** is passed at an early stage; **Jersey Tower No 4** is part of a house that blocks the promenade. If the tide is out, then drop down the sea wall to continue the walk; otherwise, move inland beforehand to continue along the main road.

There is a slipway at **Fauvic** and a plaque records how over 50 young men escaped from Jersey towards the end of the German Occupation, but in fact they left at a point a little further north. **Jersey Tower No 3** is part of a house, and the beach walk can continue if the tide allows, otherwise use the road. ▸ Around **Jersey Tower No 2** it is possible to follow another short stretch of promenade. **Jersey Tower No 1** stands on a rocky headland which can be passed only by walking along the beach at the foot of the tower, or by using the main road. The slipway before this tower leads directly to the Seymour Inn. When the tide is out, a wild and rocky area extends far into the distance. With care it can be explored – see **Walk 17**.

Note the sculpture of Harry Varden, local golfer and the first Briton to win the United States Open.

If walking along the beach, be aware of the tides and keep an eye on steps and slipways that allow access inland.

Jersey Tower and turreted house at La Rocque, where the French landed in 1781

JERSEY TOWERS

These distinctive towers occur all round the coast of Jersey, but they are particularly regular and prominent around Fauvic and La Rocque. Their design was inspired by General Conway around 1778, who drew up a plan to encircle Jersey with them. A few were completed almost immediately, with the rest being built after the Battle of Jersey in 1781. The towers were circular for strength, incorporating a magazine, living quarters and a swivel-mounted cannon on top. Thirty one Jersey Towers were built and 24 of them remain. From 1794 Martello towers were constructed around the coast.

If the tide is out and the beach is followed onwards, note that seaweed-covered rocks are slippery, and some of the pebbly beaches prove quite tiring. Inland the road is very built up, and often there is no view of the sea. Proceed according to tidal conditions and your personal preferences. It is possible to

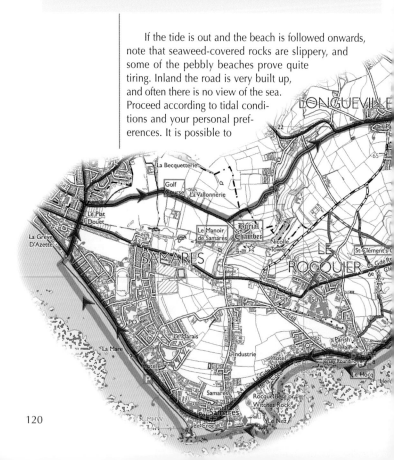

switch between options by using odd slipways linking the road and beach. There are two slipways close together, as well as a harbour wall, toilets and another Jersey Tower at **La Rocque**. ▶ The next slipway is at **Le Bourg**, then at the Pontac House Hotel at **Pontac**, followed by another one at **Le Hocq**, where there is Le Hocq Inn as well as a small grassy common, kiosk, Jersey Tower and toilets.

Take care if tempted to turn the next rocky headland as the shore is very rugged, and take care if following the road instead as it can be

The French landed at La Rocque in January 1781, marching to St Helier for the 'Battle of Jersey'.

When the tide is out splendid sandy beach walks can be enjoyed in preference to road-walking

The Green Island itself can be visited when the tide is out.

To continue walking along the coast to St Helier, follow busy roads, or the beach and short promenade paths where practical, keeping right of a prominent power station chimney to reach the harbour and town centre.

busy, passing the Shakespeare Hotel. There is an opportunity to switch between the road and shore again at **Le Croc**, or Green Island, where there is a slipway, toilets and the Green Island Restaurant. ◄ There is a shop on the coast road, followed by another slipway and toilets at **La Mare**. A prominent white girderwork lighthouse is passed, close to a shop and the Hotel Ambassadeur. At the next slipway, Grand Charrière, there is a beach café, while toilets are located in a German bunker. There are plenty of bus services here on the outskirts of St Helier. ◄ To explore inland, turn right along Plat Douet Road, walking straight through a busy crossroads at **Le Plat Douet**. Turn right along a narrow 'green lane' signposted for St Clement's Golf and Sports Centre. This road is La Blinerie and it passes sports facilities to reach quiet countryside beyond. **Samarès Manor** is a popular visitor attraction on the right, but there is no access to it or its wonderful gardens from this side.

Turn left at a road junction, along another 'green lane', and walk to a group of houses. Turn left and right in quick succession and climb up La Rue Soulas. There are

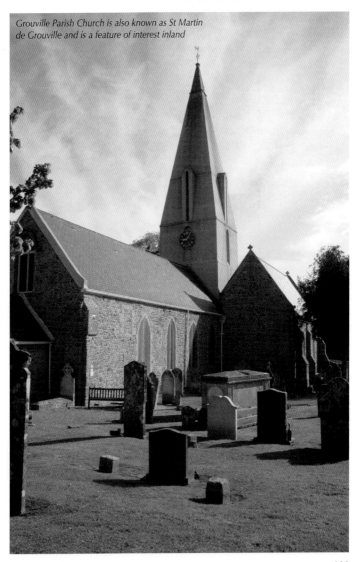

Grouville Parish Church is also known as St Martin de Grouville and is a feature of interest inland

The battle referred to in the place-name took place in 1406, when the French were assisted by a band of Spaniards.

views back towards St Helier and the road is overhung by trees later. Join a busy main road and continue straight over a rise at the village of Grouville Arsenal to reach a junction at Jardin de la Croix de la Bataille. The National Trust for Jersey owns a triangular patch of land covered in trees here. ◀

Do not go down the main road, but keep straight ahead along a minor road, La Rue des Alleurs, still rising gently through fields. The tower of an old windmill can be seen to the right, while there is a glimpse of Mont Orgueil Castle ahead. The road descends with steep, well-vegetated banks overhung with trees, and at the bottom is Grouville Parish Hall. Turn left along the main road to pass **Grouville Parish Church**.

Grouville Parish Church, also known as St Martin de Grouville, may be over 1000 years old. The ancient stone baptismal font has a particularly chequered history, having served for centuries before being thrown out of the church and used as a pig trough, then somehow finding its way up to La Hougue Bie before being reinstated as a baptismal font! There is also some fine silver altar-ware.

Follow the main road left as signposted for Gorey. Turn right at a graveyard further along the road and follow the road back to the Beausite Hotel. There are many fine buildings around this little village.

WALK 17

La Rocque and Seymour Tower

Distance	5km (3 miles)
Terrain	Entirely inter-tidal, possible only at low water during spring tides; marked by metal posts over sand, gravel, rock and slippery seaweed.
Start/Finish	Seymour Inn, La Rocque
Refreshments	Seymour Inn, La Rocque.
Transport	Bus 1 serves the Seymour Inn and La Rocque.

This is a tidal route and most of the time it simply cannot be attempted. The ideal time to cover the route is on a clear day, at low water during spring tides. With due care and attention, this is a fascinating walk, travelling far from the Jersey shore, across shoals of sand, gravel and shells, passing spiky granite reefs, rock pools and masses of seaweed. Seymour Tower is a prominent landmark – a small and completely isolated fortified tower. It is possible to be 'marooned' overnight, intentionally or by prior arrangement, as the building offers basic accommodation.

SAFETY NOTE: TIME AND TIDE WAIT FOR NO MAN!

Walking to Seymour Tower depends on a number of favourable conditions. The first requirement is a spring tide ebb, when the sea recedes furthest from the land. Second, daylight and clear weather are essential for navigation, so that route options can be seen in all directions. Third, common-sense and clear judgement is required. Do not attempt this walk barefoot, or your feet will be torn to shreds on stones and shells! The safest way to complete this walk is to set off a couple of hours before low water, in effect going out with the tide. Set off back from the tower before the turn of the tide, and there should be plenty of time to reach the shore in safety. If in doubt, do not attempt this walk at all, or play safe and hire the services of an experienced inter-tidal guide, tel. 01534 853138, mobile 07797 853033, www.jerseywalkadventures.co.uk.

Jersey Tower number 1 on a rugged little headland at La Rocque

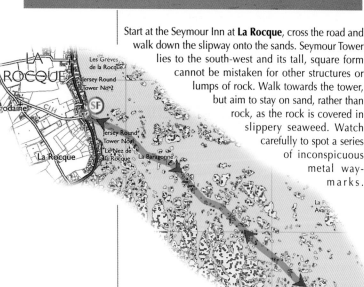

Start at the Seymour Inn at **La Rocque**, cross the road and walk down the slipway onto the sands. Seymour Tower lies to the south-west and its tall, square form cannot be mistaken for other structures or lumps of rock. Walk towards the tower, but aim to stay on sand, rather than rock, as the rock is covered in slippery seaweed. Watch carefully to spot a series of inconspicuous metal way-marks.

These are knee-high poles, painted white, with small rectangular tops, fixed to rocks along the way. They generally steer walkers across areas of sand, gravel and shells, rather than rough, rocky reefs. Looking ahead at intervals, they are generally aligned a little to the left of the tower.

Take careful note of the shape of the seabed. There is a slight downward slope from the shore, followed by a noticeable rise, reaching a slender metal tower equipped with ladders. When the tide advances the low-lying area between the metal tower and the shore floods some time **before** the area around Seymour Tower. Anyone mis-timing their return to the shore risks being cut off, and this tower is their only refuge. One can only wonder what a miserable experience it would be to be stuck on top of it for several hours!

Keep the metal marker poles in sight and follow them to **Seymour Tower**. Rugged steps lead up to a gun platform facing France, and a considerable expanse of rock and sand stretches further in that direction. A fine stretch of Jersey's coast can be seen, from St Helier to Mont Orgueil Castle. Keep an eye on the time and head back towards the shore **before** the tide turns, allowing the best possible safety margin.

Despite being square instead of round, Seymour Tower is a Jersey Tower

127

SEYMOUR TOWER

Like a square peg in a round hole, Seymour Tower is one of the late 18th century Jersey Towers; however, instead of being round, it was built square to fit the shape of the rocky outcrop it occupies. The guards who manned this remote outpost were issued with 5.5kg (12lbs) of candles per month, used to facilitate communications with other coastal lookouts. Seymour Tower is a Jersey Heritage property and it can be hired for overnight occupation by groups. The hire is conditional on being accompanied by an experienced local guide, www.jerseyheritage.org/heritage-holiday-lets.

ICHO TOWER

Icho Tower is a Martello Tower, dating from 1810, lying roughly 3km (2 miles) west of Seymour Tower in a similarly exposed tidal location. It too can be approached on foot when the tide is exceptionally low, but the journey from the Jersey shore is a little longer than that to Seymour Tower, and also rather tougher, taking longer to complete. There are no waymarks to guide walkers, and the time that can be spent at the tower before the turn of the tide is very limited.

LES MINQUIERS

When the tide recedes from La Rocque and Le Hocq, spiky reefs emerge from the water, and a huge expanse of seaweed, rocks and rock pools are exposed. The area is riddled with a maze of channels and the advancing tide is treacherous. As the area is exposed twice daily to the sun and lapped by fairly shallow waters, it is warmer than the surrounding sea and is an important area for plankton to breed, providing food for fish and everything else in the food chain. Huge numbers of wading birds probe the pools and sandy areas. The parish of Grouville extends even further than these rocky reefs, embracing the distant reef of Les Minquiers, almost halfway between Grouville and St Malo in France. Sovereignty was disputed between Jersey and France for a long time, but in 1953 the European Court upheld Jersey's claim. Jersey fishermen ensure that the reef is regularly visited.

THE BATTLE OF JERSEY

A treacherous Jerseyman showed Baron de Rullecourt and a French force how to get through the rocky reefs to La Rocque in January 1781. A plaque on the harbour wall records their landing. The French moved quickly to St Helier and compelled the Lieutenant Governor to surrender almost before he was out of bed. As news of the surrender circulated, a Yorkshireman called Major Peirson refused to capitulate and led a force against the French. The 'Battle of Jersey', as it became known, was a short, fierce engagement, resulting in the deaths of both Major Peirson and Baron de Rullecourt, and the defeat of the French force.

Leave Seymour Tower long before the sea advances towards it and return to the safety of the shore

WALK 18
La Hougue Bie and Queen's Valley

Distance	7km (4½ miles)
Terrain	Easy roads and paths throughout, in farmland and woodland.
Start/Finish	La Hougue Bie
Refreshments	Very basic refreshments at La Hougue Bie.
Transport	Bus 3a and the Green Explorer serve La Hougue Bie and St Saviour's Hospital.

La Hougue Bie is a huge Neolithic burial mound crowned by two medieval chapels outside St Helier. It is the centrepiece of a fine archaeological and geological museum in an interesting setting. After visiting this immensely absorbing site the countryside around it can be explored by following a short and simple walk. Roads must be followed at first, then well-wooded paths can be enjoyed beside the Queen's Valley Reservoir. Other quiet roads are used to climb back to La Hougue Bie afterwards.

LA HOUGUE BIE MUSEUM

La Hougue Bie is a huge, 12m (40ft) high Neolithic mound covering a long, stone-lined burial chamber, big enough to stand up inside. The medieval Chapel of Notre Dame de la Clarté and the Jerusalem Chapel crown the mound, containing interesting painted frescoes. A Battalion Command Bunker was dug into the mound during the German Occupation. A reconstruction of a Neolithic house can be inspected, and there are further exhibits in the Archaeology Museum. The Geology Museum is in another part of the building. Both museums are essential for anyone interested in the development of Jersey from the earliest times. Basic refreshments and literature are available from a little shop. La Hougue Bie is managed by Jersey Heritage, is open daily and there is an entry charge, tel. 01534 633373, www.jerseyheritage.org.

La Hougue Bie features a huge Neolithic burial mound crowned by a medieval chapel

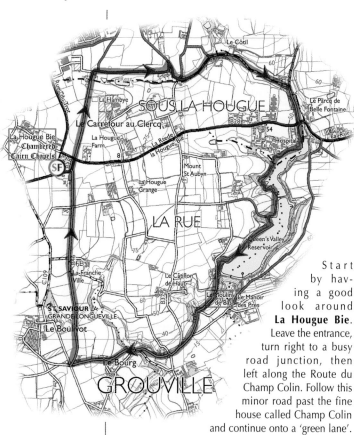

Start by having a good look around **La Hougue Bie**. Leave the entrance, turn right to a busy road junction, then left along the Route du Champ Colin. Follow this minor road past the fine house called Champ Colin and continue onto a 'green lane'. Turn right to follow Rue de Neuilly, which later bends left at Neuilly to reach a junction. Turn sharp right downhill, go through a crossroads, and continue straight along Rue St Julien. Keep following the road down through a valley, passing the farm of **Le Côtil**. The road reaches houses at La Carrièthe. Turn right here, along La Rue de la Chouquetterie, reaching a main road at the head of **Queen's Valley Reservoir**. Turn left and right to enter a car park beside a duckpond.

QUEEN'S VALLEY RESERVOIR

In 1991 Queen's Valley was flooded to form the largest reservoir on Jersey, and indeed the largest in the Channel Islands. A lovely wooded valley was lost, but a well-wooded waterside walk was created, with fishing available. The reservoir and its woods attract little grebe, tufted duck, wood warbler, woodpecker, sparrowhawk and owls. Local artists painted the valley before it was lost. A few National Trust for Jersey properties were drowned, but the Trust was given property in Fern Valley, explored during **Walk 20**, as compensation. As a result of extra water becoming available, there was an increase in the number of applications for buildings and hotel extensions around Jersey!

The well-wooded shores of Queen's Valley Reservoir are followed below St Saviour's Hospital

Walk round the duck pond at the head of the reservoir, catching a glimpse of the large buildings of **St Saviour's Hospital**. The path runs across a wooded slope below the hospital, undulating and becoming broader. A bridge is passed and views open up as the grassy dam of the reservoir is approached. Before reaching the dam, fork right up a path and go through a gate to reach a road. ▶

Walk 15 follows a path on the opposite shore of the reservoir.

An old road, no longer used by traffic, is used to climb to Le Bourg

Turn left to follow the road downhill, keeping right at the bottom, along La Rue du Moulin de Bas. Keep straight ahead at another junction, then at the next, keep right and go straight ahead between houses. Pass a big house called Springvale and follow a narrow road uphill. Turn right up an even narrower road marked 'no entry', which is too narrow and overgrown for vehicles. Climb towards a few houses at **Le Bourg** and turn right up another road, passing a house called Estralita. Later, there is a sports pitch to the left. Turn right at a junction to follow La Route de Francheville, which is signposted for La Hougue Bie. The road climbs straight uphill, passing **La Francheville** and later reaching a busy road junction beside **La Hougue Bie**.

WALK 19

La Vallée des Vaux and Les Grands Vaux

Distance	10km (6¼ miles)
Terrain	Woodland paths in valleys, giving way to roads through higher farmland.
Start/Finish	Trinity Road, St Helier
Refreshments	Plenty of choice in St Helier. Restaurant in La Vallée des Vaux.
Transport	Buses 3b, 4, 21 and 23 can be used to reach the outskirts of St Helier. Bus 4 serves the Sir Francis Cook Gallery. Bus 21 serves Victoria Village and Les Grands Vaux.

Wooded valleys converge on the northern outskirts of St Helier and a circular walk out of town and back again follows their sinuous courses. La Vallée des Vaux is followed on the outward journey – a well-wooded and steep-sided valley riddled with lovely little paths. There are opportunities to visit the Sir Francis Cook Gallery and the Eric Young Orchid Foundation. The return to St Helier by way of Les Grands Vaux is along roads; there is no access to the shore of a reservoir in the valley.

This walk starts in the northern suburbs of St Helier, where Trinity Road gives way to Trinity Hill. Several bus services use the road, and it is easily reached on foot from the centre of town. **La Vallée des Vaux** is signposted along a 'green lane' passing a supermarket. After passing The Farm, the valley road seems quiet and rural, but the suburbs above the valley continue to spread into the countryside.

The wooded slopes flanking **La Vallée des Vaux** were the first properties donated to the National Trust for Jersey, in 1937. A granite stone carved with the words 'Le Don Carlyle Le Gallais' records the original gift, which was basically two areas of woodland. Further small acquisitions were made in the valley over a number of

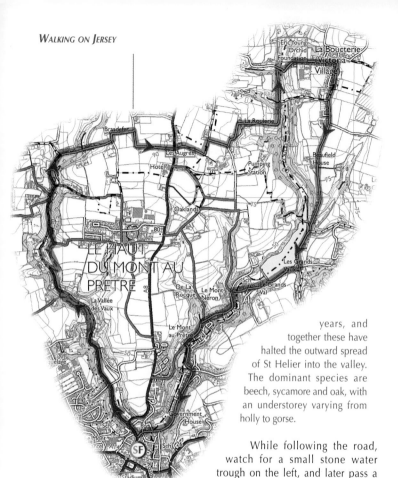

years, and
together these have
halted the outward spread
of St Helier into the valley.
The dominant species are
beech, sycamore and oak, with
an understorey varying from
holly to gorse.

While following the road,
watch for a small stone water
trough on the left, and later pass a
house called The Glen on the right. Look
across the road to spot a narrow path entering
the woods, which climbs across the slope and becomes
much clearer. It reaches a broader path and goes down it
a short way, then another path on the left is followed. Aim
to stay high on the wooded slope, above the road but
running parallel to it. Pass the top of a flight of wooden
steps then go down a flight of stout granite steps to the
road.

A flight of stout stone steps is used on a steep wooded slope in La Vallée des Vaux

Turn left to follow the road through the valley, taking note of a broadening grassy strip on the left. However, watch for another path climbing the slope on the right. The path immediately splits and either way can be taken, but heading right allows a fine loop to be enjoyed, climbing to the brow of the valley where there is a view across the tree-tops. The path drops down beside a narrow road, La Route du Petit Clos, which is followed down to the valley road again. Turn right at the bottom to pass the Harvest Barn restaurant. When a road junction is reached, walk past a pond used by ducks and geese, then turn left along the road marked as Vallée des Vaux.

Ducks and geese crowd around a small pond in the valley near the Harvest Barn restaurant

The road rises a little and crosses a river. Keep right along the Rue de Vieux Moulin, which climbs steeply later. At the top of the road, turn left, then right at **Brasdefer**, and reach another junction at the end of Rue de la Hauteur. Turn right, then left, passing potato fields to reach a crossroads at the end of Rue de la Garenne, at **Les Augrès**. At this point, the Sir Francis Cook Gallery lies off to the right, and can be visited by making a short detour.

The **Sir Francis Cook Gallery**, in a former Methodist church and school at Les Augrès, was converted into an art gallery by the late Sir Francis Cook. Some of his paintings are on permanent display and there is an extension to the old church which is used as a store-room for various works of art. The gallery has very limited opening times, so check in advance if you are keen to visit, tel. 01534 863333.

Walk through the crossroads to follow Rue de la Croiserie, which later turns left. Watch for a Route 3 cycleway marker and turn right down a road, later turning left and right at **La Roulerie** to drop into a well-wooded valley, reaching a couple of houses near a National Trust for Jersey sign for Le Pré de Ponterrin. At this point it is worth turning right uphill, watching for a gap on the right where a path enters woodland. The path soon splits, but as it forms a loop, go either way knowing that you will return along the other. One path climbs across a wooded slope while the other one stays low, near the swampy valley floor. Back on the road, walk down to the houses and turn right, following Rue au Bailli along the valley floor to a junction. Turn right, marked 'no entry' and pass the ruins of Moulin de Ponterrin. Climb steeply up the narrow road and the **Eric Young Orchid Foundation** lies to the right.

ERIC YOUNG ORCHID FOUNDATION

The late Eric Young's passion for orchids began while he was young, and increased when he bought an old market garden on Jersey and stocked it with orchids from an English nursery. After becoming a world authority on orchids, he established a dedicated centre in 1958 at an old tomato nursery at Victoria Village. He died before it was fully operational, but developments continue apace and the centre is known worldwide. There are exotic displays and the large growing houses are filled with a wide variety of tropical orchids. Access to some parts may be limited, but the Display House is fully accessible and a range of orchids are shown to their best advantage in raised beds. Plants are grown and bred, and the centre offers plenty of advice for growers. The site is generally open Wednesday to Saturday, and there is an entry charge, tel. 01534 861963, www.ericyoungorchidfoundation.co.uk.

The road continues into **Victoria Village**, where a right turn is made along La Rue de la Boucterie. Keep straight ahead at a junction beside Oaklands Manor to walk down Mont de la Rosière, dropping more steeply after passing **Beaufield House**. Follow the road alongside **Les Grands Vaux Reservoir**, turning right at a grassy corner and later following the road past the concrete dam. The road descends past the **Les Grands Vaux School** and

The Grands Vaux Reservoir is passed on the way back down towards St Helier

the rest of the valley floor is quite built up with housing, with wooded slopes rising steeply above. Bus services run through **Les Grands Vaux**, but it is not far to walk back to Trinity Road, where the walk started, and it is also possible to keep walking straight into the centre of St Helier to finish.

WALK 20
Sion and Hamptonne

Distance	11km (7 miles)
Terrain	Mostly quiet roads, with some woodland paths that are steep in some places and muddy in others.
Start/Finish	Sion Methodist Church
Refreshments	Shop at Sion. Restaurant at Hamptonne (when open).
Transport	Bus 5 serves Sion Methodist Church and bus 7 runs near Hamptonne.

This walk starts in the village of Sion and wanders along roads past the Steam, Motor and General Museum. The route then heads for the wooded Fern Valley and Waterworks Valley. Waterworks Valley, formerly known as La Vallée de St Laurens, is a gathering ground for Jersey's water. At the head of the valley is Hamptonne – a wonderful collection of old farmhouses with poignant reminders of farming traditions long past. On the return to Sion the route takes in a point believed to be the centre of Jersey.

Sion Methodist Church is an imposing building on La Grande Route de St Jean, north of St Helier. Starting from that point, follow the main road further north, passing a small cemetery, Cimitière Macapela, and the United Reformed Church. A signpost points right along a minor road, La Rue du Béchet, indicating the way to the Steam, Motor and General Museum. To reach it, pass a series of large buildings then turn right to find the museum tucked away behind them.

STEAM, MOTOR AND GENERAL MUSEUM

The late 'Don' Pallot, who founded the Steam Museum, used to work on the old Jersey Railway. The museum offers information about watermills and water turbines, as well as electricity generators and steam engines. ▶

There are steam-rollers and tractors, agricultural and domestic implements and plenty of other bits of machinery. An organ room features both church and cinema organs. A small railway station has been built, along with a circular track. Steam locos may be running, or may be visited in the engine house. Information on the layout of Jersey's old railway lines is also displayed. There is an entry charge, tel. 01534 865307, www.pallotmuseum.co.uk.

Leave the museum and turn right to continue along the Rue du Brabant. The road turns right and there is a glimpse of Le Manoir de la Trinité, or at least part

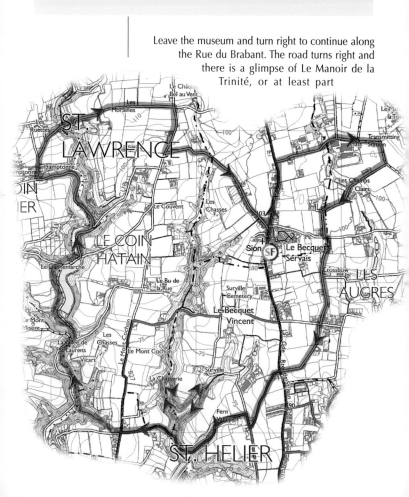

of its steep roof and tall chimneys. Turn right again along Rue des Canons, and note a little pool off to the right at a dip in the road. Turn left later at some houses and walk to the end of La Rue du Poivre, reaching a house called Mon Plaisir. Turn left and right in quick succession to follow Rue du Douet downhill. At another staggered crossroads, continue through to Rue de Haut de l'Orme. This passes Rondels Farm Shop and reaches **La Grande Route de St Jean** near the Union Inn. Cross over this busy road and follow the 'green lane' called Rue de Maupertuis. Turn right along a road marked 'no through road', which later turns left downhill and is marked 'no entry'. The road is quite narrow and runs down a grassy valley into woods, passing a damp and flowery meadow at the bottom, where there is a small reservoir. At this point, a walk around **Fern Valley** is highly recommended.

A viewpoint in Fern Valley overlooks Liberation Wood, planted in 1945

Optional Extension around Fern Valley

Turn right along a broad path, passing a National Trust for Jersey sign. The path splits, with duckboards to the left and wooden steps climbing to the right. It does not matter which way you go, as you later return to this point. However, turn left along the duckboards, climbing up and down wooden steps. Turn left at a junction of paths, later turning right in a wooded valley known as Liberation Wood, planted in 1945. Climb to a viewing platform where there is an information board. Follow the path round into another valley and go down steps. Turn left at a junction and later right into denser woods. Go up and down wooden steps to return to the broad path, and so back to the road. The additional distance is 1.5km (1 mile).

Climb steeply up the road from the reservoir, through a crossroads and down La Ruelle de St Clair. Turn right down a clear path leading into the wooded Waterworks Valley, originally named **La Vallée de St Laurens** – see Walk 21. The path later passes a stone bench beside a little bridge, continuing upstream and forking left at a path junction. The site of a mill is passed at **Vicart**, first mentioned in 1309, though little remains to be seen. The path follows a mill-race into a clearing where an information board explains about the history and natural history of the trail.

Walk through the clearing to reach a road junction near the Pine Tree Kennels. Cross the road and follow a path running parallel to the road, further up the valley. The floor of the valley may be wet, so the path uses duckboards, little footbridges and 'stepping logs'. Turn left along a broader path, climbing steps to cross a track. A long and steep flight of wooden steps climbs a wooded slope above the dam of **Dannemarche Reservoir**. A level stretch of path affords only glimpses of the reservoir, before it becomes a roller-coaster, up and down steps as it crosses the slope. ◀ Drop down through the woods to a road junction at the foot of Le Mont de Chenaie.

Turn left to follow the road beside the reservoir, then turn left again through a small rock cutting to follow a path. Cross a water channel and walk past a pool, following a woodland path, reaching another road junction and some information boards. This point was also the site of Le Moulin de la Haye, which existed from the 15th century, but nothing remains of it. Turn left to follow the path parallel to the road, crossing it later and continuing

The Moulin de Dannemarche, which once raised funds for the education of scholars, now lies beneath the reservoir.

Hamptonne Country Life Museum is well worth a visit when it features its 'event' days

HAMPTONNE COUNTRY LIFE MUSEUM

A huddle of farm buildings was bought by the National Trust for Jersey, restored at great expense, and is managed by Jersey Heritage. Opening times are limited and the site offers insights into the development of farming from the 17th to the 19th centuries. Period settings can be studied in the Langlois House, Hamptonne House, Syvret Building and the farm outbuildings. At certain times there may be people in period costume able to talk about the life and times of the farming community. There are plenty of household and agricultural implements on display, as well as a few animals roaming around the grounds, and a replanted orchard. There is an entry charge, tel. 01534 633300 for information about 'event' days, www.jerseyheritage.org.

alongside it, at the foot of a stout retaining wall. Later, the path heads right, away from the road, so leave it and follow the road, Le Chemin des Moulins, uphill. Turn right for the **Hamptonne Country Life Museum** on Rue de la Patente.

Turn right along the road when leaving Hamptonne, and right again at a small car park. Follow a narrow road downhill, which is called La Rue des Bas. At the bottom, a house on the left features a water-wheel. Climb straight up the road, Le Mont Gavey, and continue along La Rue des Moraines at the top. Later, turn right along La Rue de St Jean, which is signposted for St Helier. Turn left off this road later, walk-ing gently down La Rue des Saints

The Centre Stone is not native to its location near Sion and is said to mark the centre of Jersey

Germains, past the entrance of Les Saints Germains, then climbing gradually uphill. On the right is a boul-der known as The Centre Stone, while just beyond is La Grande Route de St Jean and **Sion Methodist Church**, where the walk started. There is a shop in the village if anything is needed before the bus arrives.

> The **Centre Stone** is a curious boulder that rests against a house near Sion. It may be all that remains of a pre-historic structure known as La Hougue Brune, and the stone itself is not from this actual locality. Many con-sider that it marks the exact centre of Jersey, so it is known as the Centre Stone.

WALK 21

Le Sentier des Moulins

Distance	7km (4¼ miles)
Terrain	Quiet roads, good tracks and paths through a well-wooded valley.
Start	Between Millbrook and La Motte
Finish	Carrefour Selous
Refreshments	Only near the start at Millbrook and La Motte.
Transport	Buses 8, 9, 12, 12a, 15 and the Red, Blue and Yellow Explorers pass Millbrook and La Motte. Bus 7 and occasionally 5 serve Carrefour Selous.

La Vallée de St Laurens slices straight through the middle of Jersey. Being steep-sided and well-watered, it was an ideal place for the construction of water mills, some of which operated for several centuries. As the valley had few habitations, it later attracted the attention of water engineers. Millbrook Reservoir was constructed during 1895 and 1896; Dannemarche Reservoir was constructed in 1909. Handois Reservoir was constructed at the top of the valley during 1931 and 1932. With the whole valley dedicated to water catchment, it is now commonly referred to as Waterworks Valley. Le Sentier des Moulins, however, recalls the bygone times of the old mills.

Start between **Millbrook** and La Motte, which are set back from the promenade between St Helier and St Aubin. The main road is used by several bus services and a minor road is signposted for Waterworks Valley. The road is called Le Chemin des Moulins and it climbs gently through a wooded valley, passing a few houses. ▶ Pass **Millbrook Reservoir** by road and note how the wooded slope to the left is maintained as a conservation area. Walk past a junction with Ruelle de St Clair and watch for a notice on the right announcing the start of 'Le Sentier des Moulins', or in *Jèrriais*, 'Le Sente des Moulîns'.

Note how the valley floor is damp and covered in rampant vegetation.

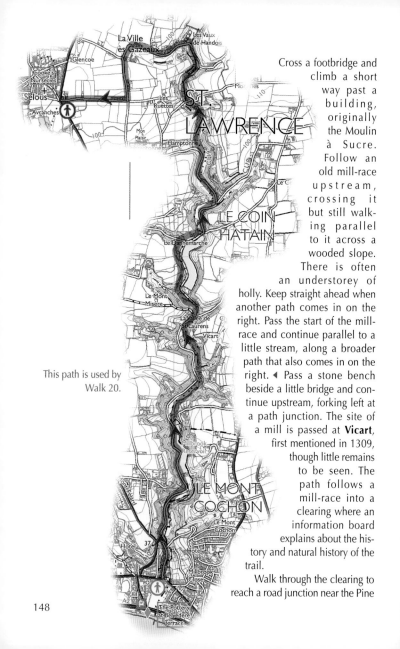

Cross a footbridge and climb a short way past a building, originally the Moulin à Sucre. Follow an old mill-race upstream, crossing it but still walking parallel to it across a wooded slope. There is often an understorey of holly. Keep straight ahead when another path comes in on the right. Pass the start of the mill-race and continue parallel to a little stream, along a broader path that also comes in on the right. ◀ Pass a stone bench beside a little bridge and continue upstream, forking left at a path junction. The site of a mill is passed at **Vicart**, first mentioned in 1309, though little remains to be seen. The path follows a mill-race into a clearing where an information board explains about the history and natural history of the trail.

Walk through the clearing to reach a road junction near the Pine

This path is used by Walk 20.

Walkers climb a steep flight of wooden steps in woods above the Dannemarche Reservoir

Le Moulin de Quétivel has been converted to a dwelling house, but it retains its water-wheel

There is no refreshment in the valley, but a concrete track climbs steeply up Le Mont Miserée to St Lawrence, which has a pub.

The Moulin de Dannemarche, which once raised funds for the education of scholars, now lies beneath the reservoir.

Tree Kennels. ◀ Cross the road and follow a path running parallel to the road, further up the valley. The floor of the valley may be wet, so the path uses duckboards, little foot-bridges and 'stepping logs'. Turn left along a broader path, climbing steps to cross a track. A long and steep flight of wooden steps climbs a wooded slope above the dam of **Dannemarche Reservoir**. A level stretch of path affords only glimpses of the reservoir, before the path becomes a roller-coaster, up and down steps as it crosses the slope. ◀ Drop down through the woods to a road junction at the foot of Le Mont de Chenaie.

Turn left to follow the road beside the reservoir, then turn left again through a small rock cutting to follow a path. Cross a water channel and walk past a pool, following a woodland path, reaching another road junction and some information boards. This point was also the site of Le Moulin de la Haye, which existed from the 15th century, but nothing remains of it. Turn left to follow the path parallel to the road, crossing it later and continuing alongside it, at the foot of a stout retaining wall. Later, the path heads right, away from the road, while the road is used by **Walk 20** to reach nearby **Hamptonne**.

Follow the valley path through woods, cross a footbridge and walk though a tiny field to reach yet another road junction. Go straight ahead along a narrow road, La Rue Ville ès Gazeau, with a duckpond to the right and Le Moulin de Quétivel to the left. The mill has been converted into a dwelling, but features a working waterwheel. Just as the road begins to bend right, another path runs parallel to it, crossing a little stream twice in quick succession. A final information board is reached at Handois, explaining how the area used to be known as China Quarries, after china clay was extracted, and also tells the chilling tale of a ghostly procession!

There is no further access up through Waterworks Valley, and the way ahead is blocked by the dam of Handois Reservoir. To finish, leave the valley by walking up La Rue Ville ès Gazeau, keeping straight ahead at the top along La Rue de la Hauteur. Later, turn right at a crossroads along Rue Parcqthée, reaching a busy road junction with bus services at **Carrefour Selous**.

WALK 22
St Peter's Valley

Distance	9km (5½ miles)
Terrain	Woodland paths at the start, giving way to quiet road walking.
Start/Finish	Jersey War Tunnels
Refreshments	Cafés at the Jersey War Tunnels and Jersey's Living Legend Village.
Transport	Bus 8 runs along St Peter's Valley. Bus 8a and the Red and Yellow Explorers link the Jersey War Tunnels and Jersey's Living Legend Village.

This walk runs through wooded valleys and crosses the high ground between them, taking advantage of paths where they exist, otherwise using quiet roads. The Jersey War Tunnels can be explored at the beginning or end of the walk. Le Moulin de Quétivel is passed while walking through St Peter's Valley. Another major visitor site is Jersey's Living Legend Village. A number of National Trust for Jersey properties can be seen in a quiet area of countryside between St Matthew and St Lawrence. While the distance is short, the visitor attractions could take all day to explore!

JERSEY WAR TUNNELS

Known to the Germans as 'Ho8' (*Höhlgangsanlage 8*) these tunnels were originally for storage and were later converted into an underground hospital. The tunnel system is extensive and different passages and rooms explore different themes. Visitors can wander through at their own pace, and there are plenty of displays along the way. The tunnels were hacked from Jersey shale by foreign slave workers under the direction of Organisation Todt. Harrowing stories of the tunnel's construction and of the German Occupation are graphically illustrated. The tunnels are open daily, March to November, and there is an entry charge, tel. 01534 860808, www.jerseywartunnels.com. A shop and restaurant can be visited for free and the walls commemorate islanders who resisted the occupying forces, were deported or otherwise suffered or died. The information was collected by a past curator, Joe Miére. Out in the open a 'War Trail' can be followed. This path network leads through woods and passes trenches, gun emplacements and other defence structures.

Leave the **Jersey War Tunnels** and walk down its access road to a bus stop. Almost immediately, off to the right, is a 'War Trail' sign indicating a path up a wooded slope. ▶ There is a brief view from the top, down through the wooded valley, to the sea at St Aubin's Bay.

Take care to keep to the left on the way downhill.

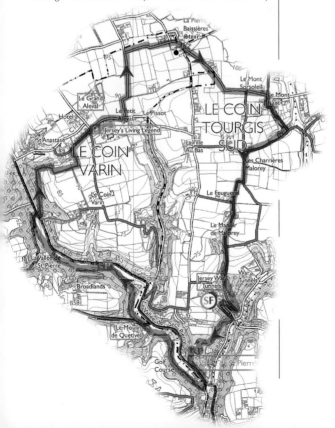

153

Tesson Mill is a National Trust for Jersey property and has a water-wheel around the back

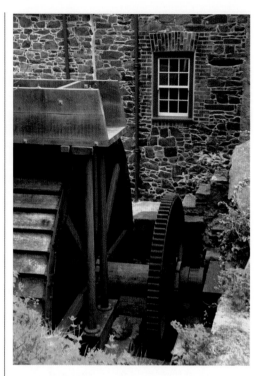

Follow the path downhill as signposted to reach a busy main road in St Peter's Valley, or **La Vallée de St Pierre**.

Cross the road and turn left, following a path parallel to the road. Turn right at a road junction to pass the old Tesson Mill which is a National Trust for Jersey property. Turn right again to follow a tarmac path rising behind the mill, marked with a National Trust sign. The path becomes gravel, then keep right at a junction, running parallel to a mill-race on a wooded slope. Cross a road to reach **Le Moulin de Quétivel**.

Le Moulin de Quétivel watermill is a National Trust for Jersey property, which is sometimes open on Saturdays,

A track runs past woodlands and fields towards Jersey's Living Legend Village

and there is an entry charge. The millwheel is in full working order. There is information about milling and bread making, as well as a fine reconstruction of an old Jersey kitchen and a small herb garden.

Climb up some stone steps behind the mill to continue through St Peter's Valley. After passing through a car park, more steps climb a little higher onto a wooded slope. These slopes are Les Côtils Don Gaudin, and are another National Trust property. Climb a little further but later keep right on the most well-trodden path downhill to emerge at a millpond close to the main road. Continue along a narrow path beside the main road. ▶ Continue this way until a road junction is reached opposite Gargate House.

Generally, there is a row of trees between the busy traffic and the path users.

Walk back a few paces along the main road then turn left along a 'green lane' behind Gargate House, called Mont des Ruelles, also marked as cycleway Route 6A. A woodland track rises steeply then you turn left along a woodland path. ▶ The track is bendy as it levels out beside fields. When a tarmac road is joined, turn right to follow it to **Jersey's Living Legend Village**.

Listen for woodpeckers while passing through.

155

Jersey's Living Legend Village is free to visit, but there is a charge for the Jersey Experience

JERSEY'S LIVING LEGEND VILLAGE

A craft and shopping village has been created around courtyards enlivened by flower beds, with food and drink readily available. The Jersey Experience is an added entertainment, open daily March to October, more limited at other times and closed in mid-winter, for which there is an entry charge, tel. 01534 485496, www.jerseyslivinglegend.co.je. The 'experience' features hi-tech equipment and elaborate surroundings. As people progress through this part of the centre the history and heritage of Jersey is related by famous actors. It leads ultimately to the mythical, sunken Manoir de la Brecquette.

Leave the Village and turn right along La Rue du Petit l'Aleval. Turn left up a road signposted for St Matthieu, along La Rue des Aix, then turn right along Rue Bechervaise to reach **St Matthew's Roman Catholic Church**. ▶ Turn right at the church to face a road junction with a National Trust for Jersey sign for Le Don Marie. Keep to the left, following La Rue des Bessières gently downhill. The road is lined with trees and the enclosing banks are quite flowery. Pass a big house called Eden Grove. Walk straight through a crossroads, along **Le Mont Sorsoleil**, and later turn right down **Le Mont Isaac**, past a thatched house.

Turn left to visit a couple of interesting National Trust for Jersey properties. These include a stone water trough on the left at La Fontaine de St Martin, Le Côtil de la Qualité on the right and the delightful little Jersey cottage of Le Rât on the left. Retrace your steps back along the road and climb straight up Rue de la Fontaine St Martin, passing La Fontaine Farm to climb to the National Trust's Morel Farm. ▶ Turn left onto **Les Charrières Malorey**. The road later bends right and left at a junction, marked as cycleway Route 4, then drops downhill and passes the gateways of **Le Manoir de Malorey**. The road zigzags towards the end, and at the bottom junction a right turn leads back to the **Jersey War Tunnels**.

Large buildings stand unused in this area, which always seems sombre and quiet.

Morel Farm was founded in 1666 and features a host of quaint features, including an apple press and bakehouse.

WALK 23
St Peter's and Le Val de la Mare

Distance	10km (6¼ miles)
Terrain	Mostly roads, with some easy tracks and paths. Some of the roads are quite steep.
Start/Finish	St Peter's village
Refreshments	Pub and cafés in St Peter's village.
Transport	Bus 9 and occasionally bus 15 serve St Peter's village, while bus 8 and the Red and Yellow Explorers run through St Peter's Valley.

St Peter's village occupies an area of high ground in the west of Jersey, not far from the airport. In fact, the airport is wholly within the parish. The village is flanked on two sides by wooded valleys, both of which are gathering grounds for reservoirs. This walk leaves St Peter's village and heads for the fringe of Les Mielles. Le Val de la Mare Reservoir and an arboretum can be visited afterwards. The route then runs to the head of St Peter's Valley before climbing back up to the village.

> **St Peter's Bunker** stands beside St Peter's Country Inn and was once run as a visitor attraction, but is now closed. Stout-walled underground rooms were built during the German Occupation, and the bunker was a major command centre which controlled a host of defensive structures around St Ouen's Bay.

There are bus stops at St Peter's Country Inn in the village of St Peter's.

Walk along Rue de l'Église, passing **St Peter's Church** to reach the school. Turn right opposite the school to follow La Rue du Bocage, marked as cycleway Route 6, and continue through a crossroads to follow La Rue des Nièmes. Turn left at the next crossroads to follow a 'green lane' called Rue de la Presse away from **La Presse**.

The Bethesda Methodist Church, with Les Mielles and St Ouen's Bay beyond

The road runs along and gently downhill through potato fields. There is a view of the airport to the left, then keep right of **Le Mont de la Mare**. Follow a track out past fields, crossing another track, but do

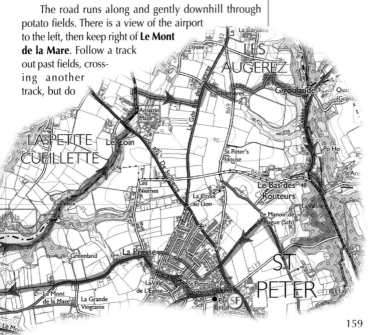

A fine house is glimpsed after climbing from woods above Le Val de la Mare Reservoir

not walk to the house called Eagle Rock. Instead, turn left down a narrow path on a slope of burnt gorse, overlooking Les Mielles and the broad sweep of St Ouen's Bay. Turn right along a road at the bottom to pass the **Bethesda Methodist Church**, go under a concrete bridge and turn right.

Walk 6 uses a path on the opposite shore.

Walk through a gate and follow a track towards the concrete dam of **Le Val de la Mare Reservoir**. Climb to the right of the dam on a zigzag path, but do not cross the dam at the top. ◄ Follow a clear gravel path alongside the reservoir, which weaves in and out and becomes more wooded as it proceeds. ◄ Walk past another gate to follow a gravel track further up a well-wooded valley, **Les Vaux**. Alternatively, cross a footbridge to follow a path running a little higher, but parallel to the track, across a wooded slope.

Look out for little grebes and reed warblers.

> There are several species of **trees** present, and it comes as no surprise to learn that this area is actually an arboretum. A stone records, 'The creation of this arboretum was inspired and funded by the late Nigel Moores for the enjoyment of the people of Jersey.'

There is a car park and a main road at the top of the valley, and a fine house across the road. A direct line could be taken back to St Peter's village, but quieter roads are to be preferred.

Turn left along the main road, the **Grande Route de St Pierre**, then turn right along La Verte Rue, climbing gently uphill. ▶ Turn right along La Rue du Pont au Bré, then left along a busier road to reach a fine roadside waterpump. Turn right at this point, along Rue d'Auvergne, then turn left at the end, marked as cycleway Route 3. A right turn along La Rue des Charrières leads gradually downhill, then drops more steeply as it winds down past Les Charrières Country Hotel, along Le Mont des Charrières. ▶ As a right turn is made at the bottom, within earshot of a large quarry, note a little mill wheel beside a small stream at **Gigoulande**.

Keep to the right when following the main road through **La Vallée**, St Peter's Valley, passing a charming little reservoir in a wooded setting. Turn left down La Rue du Moulin de la Hague. Turn right up a road, cross the main road and go through a gateway marked 'footpath'. Climb a bit and turn left down a few steps. Either follow a path through the wooded valley, parallel to the road, or climb up another path which makes a loop on the wooded slope and later descends to join the valley path. The upper path runs through more mixed woodland and is often flanked by bamboo and flowers.

Whichever route is chosen, turn right later and follow another path uphill, parallel to a minor road, still in the woods. Cross the road later and keep climbing,

The route goes past 'aMaizin Maze', which offers activities primarily aimed at young families.

The roadside banks are profusely vegetated and overhung with trees.

A fine monumental roadside pump is passed as the route turns onto Rue d'Auvergne

Jersey cows are seen grazing in the fields across the island.

emerging to walk alongside a field. Reach a crossroads at the entrance to St George's Preparatory School, based at **Le Manoir de la Hague**. La Route du Manoir could be followed straight to St Peter's, but walk instead along the road beside the wall surrounding the school grounds. A left turn leads along a 'green lane' appropriately called Verte Rue. The spire of St Peter's Church can be seen to the left, and at the end of the road a left turn leads straight back into the village.

WALK 24
Corbière Walk

Distance	6km (3¾ miles)
Terrain	A broad and clear track, rising and falling gently, usually with trees alongside.
Start	St Aubin's Harbour
Finish	La Corbière
Refreshments	Plenty around St Aubin's Harbour and off-route at Red Houses. Restaurant at La Corbière.
Transport	Bus 12 and the Blue Explorer link St Aubin and La Corbière.

A railway line was opened from St Helier to St Aubin's Harbour in 1870, along the promenade as covered in **Walk 2**. The line was extended piecemeal beyond St Aubin's Harbour and by 1899 it reached La Corbière. This extension offers a fine, traffic-free footpath and cycleway through south-west Jersey, flanked by trees most of the way. At La Corbière, if the tide is out, the walk can be extended further across a tidal causeway to a prominent little lighthouse.

JERSEY RAILWAY & TRAMWAY COMPANY

The Jersey Railway & Tramway Company opened a line from St Helier to St Aubin in 1870. The piecemeal extensions beyond St Aubin eventually reached La Corbière in 1899. Stations and halts around St Aubin's Bay included The Weighbridge, West Park, Bellozanne Halt, First Tower, Millbrook Halt, Millbrook, Bel Royal, Bel Royal Halt, Beaumont, Beaumont Halt, La Haule and St Aubin. Stations on the extended line included Pont Marquet, Don Bridge, Blanches Banques, La Moye and La Corbière. The Terminus Hotel at St Aubin, now the Salle Paroissiale de St Brelade, was destroyed by fire in 1936 and the railway, never a commercial success, was closed as a result. The line was briefly restored in 1941 during the German Occupation, and extended with narrow-gauge tracks to quarries ▶

The Corbière Walk is broad and clear, following the track-bed of the former Jersey Railway

and construction sites. The Germans also laid a line from Pont Marquet to the quarry at Ronez (**see Walk 10**), with another link to St Ouen's Bay. The whole system was dismantled in 1946.

Leave **St Aubin** from the Salle Paroissiale de St Brelade. Cross the road and keep to the right of the NatWest Bank to follow a road signposted for the Corbière Walk. An old tunnel lies just to the left of the track, used for storing oxygen and bicycles! Leaving St Aubin behind, the surroundings feature a wide variety of trees, shrubs and flowering plants, making it feel like a jungle trek. A stone at a junction between a minor and main road commemorates the opening of the Route de St Brelade.

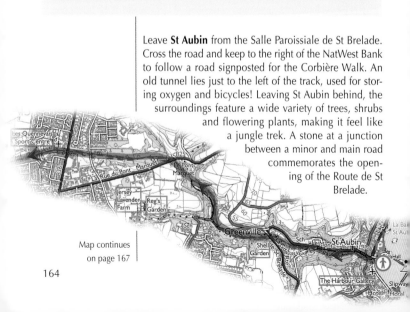

Map continues on page 167

*Exotic trees and shrubs flank the Corbière
Walk as it climbs away from St Aubin*

Havre
Sc
oin

Walkers and cyclists need to keep a lookout for each other on the Corbière Walk

The track-bed rises gently and drifts away from the main road, which is later carried overhead on a tall arch. The surroundings remain leafy as the walk passes through **Greenville**; then the next stretch is quieter. ▶ A busy road is crossed as the track-bed enters the Pont Marquet Country Park, passing a couple of reedy duck-ponds. This area is important for birds like serin, and kingfishers may sometimes be seen. The suburbs of **Les Quennevais** become apparent as a minor road is crossed. The Lavender Farm and its café lie off-route to the left. The track-bed passes under a main road at Don Bridge, where food, drink and bus services are easily reached.

Out of sight above the arch is the popular Shell Garden, where a million sea shells have been used to create fine designs.

Still rising gently, the Corbière Walk passes **Les Quennevais Sports Centre** with rows of fine pine trees on both sides. ▶ After passing the Centre the track-bed starts descending gently, and the houses alongside take a step back. La Moye Golf Club lies to the right, while a practice field lies to the left, known as the President's Field. Two narrow roads are crossed in quick succession, then the track-bed features a greater variety of trees. After crossing a couple of busy roads, there are fields and farmhouses alongside, while lines of pine trees feature again.

A variety of sports take place at the Centre, from football to petanque.

A number of little access tracks and narrow roads cross the Corbière Walk, serving farms and houses. The Highlands Hotel is seen away to the left, then a platform and modernised station building stand at the end of the track-bed at **La Corbière**. There are toilets across the road, while Le Nid de Corneilles offers food and drink. Buses can be caught beside the old station building.

Extension to La Corbière Lighthouse
The walk can be extended to the nearby lighthouse, if the tide is out and the causeway is uncovered. The walk there and back is 1.5km (1 mile). See **Walk 4** for details.

WALK 25

Jersey Coastal Walk

Distance	78.5km (48½ miles)
Terrain	Almost entirely coastal, including busy and quiet roads, as well as tracks and paths, ranging from urban areas to cliff-tops, sand dunes to woods and commons. Beach walking is an option, depending on the tides.
Start/Finish	Liberation Square, St Helier
Refreshments	Pubs, restaurants, cafés, kiosks and shops are available at many points around the coast.
Transport	All the bus services on Jersey start and finish at St Helier and all of them reach the coast at some point on their journeys.

There is no doubt that most of the best scenery on Jersey is around the coast. Naturally, many walkers feel obliged to concentrate their explorations along the coastline, and fortunately there is good access almost all the way. Once a year, in the middle of summer, there is an organised charity walk around the entire coast of the island. As the coast is well-served by bus routes, walkers with plenty of time to spare can split the distance over three, four or more days and take the time to enjoy the experience.

A complete route description is not necessary here, as the coastal route is described a stretch at a time, in a clockwise direction, ranging from **Walk 2** to **Walk 16** through this guidebook. However, the following notes help to join all the short sections together, and each daily stage can be planned simply by adding up several short stretches to reach a distance that is comfortable and achievable each day. The assumption is that you will start from St Helier, walk in a clockwise direction round the coast, and finish back in town. However, as the route is circular, any point can serve for the start

and finish, and there is no bar on walking anti-clock-wise, except all the route directions would need to be reversed. Bear in mind that any optional extensions mentioned increase the distance, and some may be dependent on the tides.

Le Grand Étacquerel in north-west Jersey, where gentle St Ouen's Bay gives way to rugged cliffs

A leisurely four-day walk around the coast could start at St Helier and be split at La Pulente, La Grève de Lecq and Bouley Bay. Bus services allow easy exits from the route and an easy return the following day. In the middle of summer, Itex and the Rotary Club organise a gruelling one-day walk around the coast of Jersey, attracting over a thousand walkers, although only 50 per cent actually finish!

Walk 2 St Helier to St Aubin
5km (3 miles)
Start at Liberation Square in St Helier and follow the route as described all the way round St Aubin's Bay to St Aubin's Harbour. Extensions to Elizabeth Castle and St Aubin's Fort are optional and dependent on favourable tides.

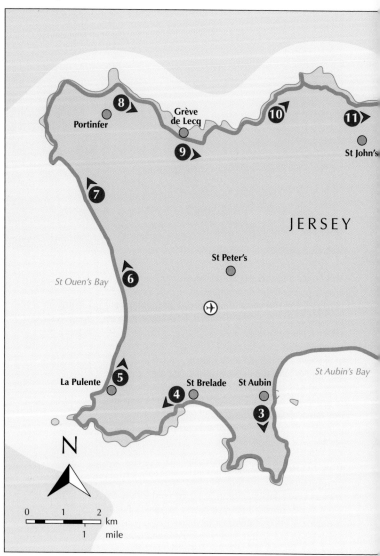

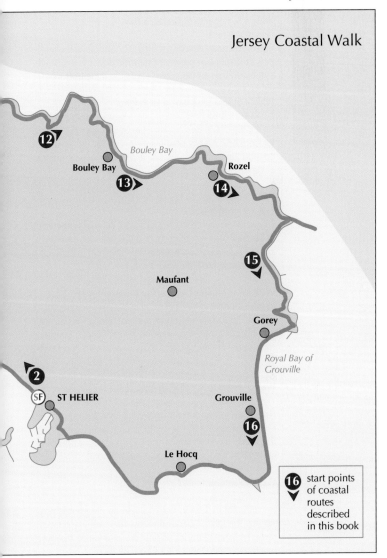

Jersey Coastal Walk

Bouley Bay

Bouley Bay

Rozel

Maufant

Gorey

Royal Bay of Grouville

ST HELIER

Grouville

Le Hocq

16 start points of coastal routes described in this book

Walk 3 St Aubin to St Brelade's Bay
7km (4½ miles)
Follow the route description from St Aubin to St Brelade's Bay. At Portelet an optional extension down to the beach and out to L'Île au Guerdain is possible if the tide is out.

Walk 4 St Brelade's Bay to La Pulente
7km (4½ miles)
Follow the route description from St Brelade's Church to La Corbière. An optional extension to the lighthouse is possible only at when the tide is out; otherwise continue as described to La Pulente.

Walk 5 La Pulente to Les Mielles Golf Course
2.5km (1½ miles)
Follow the route description from La Pulente to the café at Le Braye, then continue along the sea wall, or beach, around St Ouen's Bay. An optional extension to La Rocco Tower is only possible when the tide is out.

Walk 6 Les Mielles Golf Course to Lewis Tower
3km (2 miles)
Follow the route description and walk along the sea wall around St Ouen's Bay, passing Kempt Tower, continuing to the Channel Islands Military Museum and Lewis Tower.

Walk 7 Lewis Tower to Plémont
7km (4½ miles)
Follow the route description from Lewis Tower, past Le Grand Étacquerel at the northern end of St Ouen's Bay, then onto the cliff path around the north-east corner of Jersey. Pass Grosnez Castle to reach Plémont.

Walk 8 Plémont to La Grève de Lecq
4km (2½ miles)
An optional extension onto La Tête de Plémont is possible at the start, otherwise follow the route description directly from Plémont, along the cliff path, heading inland later and down to La Grève de Lecq.

Walk 9 La Grève de Lecq to La Falaise
5km (3 miles)
Follow the route description, first inland from La Grève de Lecq, then along a splendid cliff path to La Falaise. An optional extension at the end, which is highly recommended, is down to Devil's Hole and back uphill again.

Walk 10 La Falaise to La Cocagne
5km (3 miles)
Follow the route description from La Falaise, along the cliffs to Sorel, then along a road to pass a large quarry at Ronez. Continue along the road, La Route du Nord, to reach La Cocagne.

Walk 11 La Cocagne to Les Platons
4km (2½ miles)
Follow the route description from La Cocagne, around the cliffs to Bonne Nuit Bay. While not a coastal walk, the circular La Vallette Walk is highly recommended as an optional extra; otherwise climb to Les Platons.

Jersey's north coast features rugged headlands and secluded bays, such as Bonne Nuit Bay

The eastern coast of Jersey, looking across St Catherine's Bay from Archirondel

Walk 12 Les Platons to Bouley Bay
5km (3 miles)
Follow the route description from Les Platons, around the cliffs of La Belle Hougue, and down to Le Petit Port. Climb and follow another cliff path and drop down to Bouley Bay.

Walk 13 Bouley Bay to Rozel
5km (3 miles)
Follow the route description from Bouley Bay, along a particularly winding and undulating cliff path to reach La Tour de Rozel. Head inland by road and drop down to Rozel, possibly making a detour to the harbour.

Walk 14 Rozel to St Catherine's Tower
5km (3 miles)
Follow the route description from Rozel to St Catherine's Breakwater, with significant detours away from the coast. The breakwater offers an optional extension; otherwise follow the coast onwards to St Catherine's Tower.

Walk 15 St Catherine's Tower to Fort Henry
5km (3 miles)
Follow the route description from St Catherine's Tower to Archirondel and Anne Port, then take the road to Mont Orgueil Castle. Follow the promenade away from the harbour and then the sea wall or beach past Fort Henry.

Walk 16 Fort Henry to St Helier
9km (5½ miles)
Follow the route description from Fort Henry, around the south-eastern corner of Jersey. Road-walking is necessary most of the time if the tide is in. Continue beyond Grand Charrière to return to St Helier.

THE ITEX–ROTARY AROUND THE ISLAND WALK

This one-day event is held in the middle of summer and has been organised since 1991. In that year it was solely organised by Itex and there were only 15 participants. As the event grew over the years, the Rotary Club joined forces to help with the organisation. Walkers raise funds for charity, and these days well over 1000 people set off to complete the distance, though only half of them will actually finish. The route is more or less the same as outlined above, except it runs in an anti-clockwise direction, with a slightly different start and finish in St Helier. See www.itexwalk.je.

SPRING/AUTUMN WALKING WEEKS

During the Spring Walking Week and the Autumn Walking Week visiting walkers can join local walkers and be led by knowledgeable guides. Five-day circuits around the coast of Jersey are available, walking in an anti-clockwise direction, travelling out and back on specially-hired coaches. Dates and other arrangements can be checked on the Jersey Tourism website, www.jersey.com and there are printed booklets covering both events.

APPENDIX A
The Channel Islands Way

The Channel Islands Way was the happy inspiration of a flute-playing trio on Jersey, while enjoying a meal and good red wine after practising together in 2005. Jennifer Bridge had enjoyed a series of walks during one of the Jersey Walking Weeks, all of them led by Blue Badge guide Arthur Lamy, while Andrew Goodyear and Anna Heuston had enjoyed a trek along the celebrated West Highland Way in Scotland. As the wine flowed and their conversation developed, they agreed that a long-distance, island-hopping Channel Islands Way would be a truly remarkable route. A few years later, the idea was put to tourism bodies around the islands and was received with enthusiasm.

The mapping and a route description was prepared by Arthur Lamy. A guidebook has been published by Coast, and a dedicated Channel Islands Way website is also planned. The route envisages walkers making an anti-clockwise circuit round the coast of Jersey, and clockwise circuits round the coasts of Guernsey, Alderney, Sark and Herm. The coastlines of the two largest islands can be walked in a day by the most determined of walkers, but three or four days each allows time to enjoy the scenery and explore some of the features along the way. The

Walking the Channel Islands Way leads walkers onwards around the coast of Guernsey

Channel Islands Way walkers visit the heavily fortified island of Alderney

smaller islands can be walked around in a day apiece, although two days on Alderney and Sark would allow a much more leisurely appreciation.

So, an average long-distance walker might expect to spend a week-and-a-half walking round the coasts and hopping from island to island, covering 178km (110 miles). If the Channel Islands Way is attempted over a two-week holiday, there would be plenty of time to enjoy the route without feeling the need to dash from one island to another. The entire coastline of Jersey is covered in this guidebook, while the coastlines of Guernsey, Alderney, Sark and Herm are covered in a companion volume, *Walking on Guernsey*. The only other planning materials required would be up-to-date timetables for ferries and flights between the islands and a schedule aimed at making the best use of time. A basic table of distances is outlined below:

Walk	Distance
Jersey	77km (48 miles)
Guernsey	60km (37 miles)
Alderney	19km (11½ miles)
Sark	16km (10 miles)
Herm	6km (4 miles)
Channel Islands Way	178km (110½ miles)

The Channel Islands Way includes coastal walks around the Isle of Sark

APPENDIX B

Route summary table

No	Start	Finish	Distance
1	Liberation Square, St Helier	Liberation Square, St Helier	Variable
2	Liberation Square, St Helier	St Aubin's Harbour	5km (3 miles)
3	St Aubin's Harbour	St Aubin's Harbour	12km (7½ miles)
4	St Brelade's Bay	St Brelade's Bay	10km (6¼ miles)
5	La Pulente	La Pulente	5km (3 miles)
6	Kempt Tower, Les Mielles	Kempt Tower, Les Mielles	8km (5 miles)
7	Lewis Tower, near L'Étacq	Lewis Tower, near L'Étacq	11km (7 miles)
8	Portinfer	Portinfer	8km (5 miles)
9	La Grève de Lecq	La Grève de Lecq	12km (7½ miles)
10	The Priory Inn, La Falaise	The Priory Inn, La Falaise	10km (6¼ miles)
11	St John's Parish Church	St John's Parish Church	8km (5 miles)
12	Les Platons	Les Platons	10km (6¼ miles)

Looking back round Bonne Nuit Bay to the headland of La Tête de Frémont (Walk 11)

No	Start	Finish	Distance
13	Bouley Bay	Bouley Bay	10km (6¼ miles)
14	Rozel Harbour	Rozel Harbour	11km (7 miles)
15	St Catherine's Tower	St Catherine's Tower	13km (8 miles)
16	Grouville Station	Grouville Station	13km (8 miles)
17	Seymour Inn, La Rocque	Seymour Inn, La Rocque	5km (3 miles)
18	La Hougue Bie	La Hougue Bie	7km (4½ miles)
19	Trinity Road, St Helier	Trinity Road, St Helier	10km (6¼ miles)
20	Sion Methodist Church	Sion Methodist Church	11km (7 miles)
21	Between Millbrook and La Motte	Carrefour Selous	7km (4¼ miles)
22	Jersey War Tunnels	Jersey War Tunnels	9km (5½ miles)
23	St Peter's village	St Peter's village	10km (6¼ miles)
24	St Aubin's Harbour	La Corbière	6km (3¾ miles)
25	Liberation Square, St Helier	Liberation Square, St Helier	78.5km (48½ miles)

Looking along the cliffs of the north coast before
heading inland to St John's (Walk 10)

APPENDIX C
Contacts

Government
States of Jersey, www.gov.je
States Assembly, www.statesassembly.gov.je
Jersey Legal Information Board, www.jerseylaw.je

Tourist information
Jersey Tourism, Liberation Place, St Helier, JE1 1BB, tel. 01534 448800, email info@jersey.com, website www.jersey.com

History and heritage
Jersey Museum, The Weighbridge, St Helier, JE2 3NG, tel. 01534 633300
Jersey Heritage, contact via the museum, www.jerseyheritage.org
La Société Jersiaise, tel. 01534 758314, www.societe-jersiaise.org
National Trust for Jersey, The Elms, La Chève Rue, St Mary, Jersey, JE3 3EN, tel. 01534 483193, www.nationaltrustjersey.org.je
Channel Islands Occupation Society, www.ciosjersey.org.uk

Air travel
Flybe, tel. 0871 7002000, www.flybe.com
Bmibaby, tel. 0905 8282828, www.bmibaby.com
Blue Islands, tel. 08456 202122, www.blueislands.com
Aurigny, tel. 01481 822886, www.aurigny.com
Palmair, tel. 01202 200700, www.palmair.co.uk
Channel Islands Travel Service, tel. 01534 496600, www.jerseytravel.com

Ferry travel
Condor, tel. 0845 6091024, www.condorferries.co.uk
Manche Îles Express, tel. 01534 880756, www.manche-iles-express.com

Bus services
Connex 'myBus' and 'Explorer', Liberation Station, tel. 01534 877772, www.mybus.je

Communications
Jersey Telecom, www.jerseytelecom.com
Jersey Post, www.jerseypost.com

Map and map sales
States of Jersey 1:25,000 Official Leisure Map of Jersey
Digimap, Jersey, tel. 01534 769069, www.digimap.je
Stanfords, tel. 0207 8361321, www.stanfords.co.uk
The Map Shop, tel. 0800 0854080, www.themapshop.co.uk
Cordee, tel. 01455 611185, www.cordee.co.uk

Food and drink
Jersey Royal potatoes, www.jerseyroyals.co.uk
Jersey dairy products, www.jerseydairy.je
Jersey wines and fine foods, www.lamarewineestate.com

Emergency Contacts
Police, ambulance, fire and coastguard services, tel. 999 or 112
Jersey Honorary Police, www.jerseyhonorarypolice.org
Channel Islands Air Search, www.ci-airsearch.com

The inland parts of Jersey feature plenty of interest, such as the National Trust of Jersey's Fern Valley

FERN VALLEY

NOTES

NOTES

NOTES

NOTES

LISTING OF CICERONE GUIDES

Tour of the Vanoise
Trekking in the Vosges and Jura
Vanoise Ski Touring
Walking in Provence
Walking in the Cathar Region
Walking in the Cevennes
Walking in the Dordogne
Walking in the Haute Savoie North & South
Walking in the Languedoc
Walking in the Tarentaise and Beaufortain Alps
Walking on Corsica

GERMANY

Germany's Romantic Road
Walking in the Bavarian Alps
Walking in the Harz Mountains
Walking the River Rhine Trail

HIMALAYA

Annapurna: A Trekker's Guide
Bhutan
Everest: A Trekker's Guide
Garhwal and Kumaon: A Trekker's and Visitor's Guide
Kangchenjunga: A Trekker's Guide
Langtang with Gosainkund and Helambu: A Trekker's Guide
Manaslu: A Trekker's Guide
The Mount Kailash Trek

IRELAND

Irish Coastal Walks
The Irish Coast to Coast Walk
The Mountains of Ireland

ITALY

Gran Paradiso
Italy's Sibillini National Park
Shorter Walks in the Dolomites
Through the Italian Alps
Trekking in the Apennines
Trekking in the Dolomites
Via Ferratas of the Italian Dolomites: Vols 1 & 2
Walking in Sicily
Walking in the Central Italian Alps
Walking in the Dolomites
Walking in Tuscany
Walking on the Amalfi Coast

MEDITERRANEAN

Jordan – Walks, Treks, Caves, Climbs and Canyons
The Ala Dag
The High Mountains of Crete
The Mountains of Greece
Treks and Climbs in Wadi Rum, Jordan
Walking in Malta
Western Crete

NORTH AMERICA

British Columbia
The Grand Canyon
The John Muir Trail
The Pacific Crest Trail

SOUTH AMERICA

Aconcagua and the Southern Andes
Torres del Paine

SCANDINAVIA

Trekking in Greenland
Walking in Norway

SLOVENIA, CROATIA AND MONTENEGRO

The Julian Alps of Slovenia
The Mountains of Montenegro
Trekking in Slovenia
Walking in Croatia

SPAIN AND PORTUGAL

Costa Blanca Walks
1 West
2 East
Mountain Walking in Southern Catalunya
The Mountains of Central Spain
Trekking through Mallorca
Via de la Plata
Walking in Madeira
Walking in Mallorca
Walking in the Algarve
Walking in the Canary Islands
2 East
Walking in the Cordillera Cantabrica
Walking in the Sierra Nevada
Walking on La Gomera and El Hierro
Walking on La Palma
Walking the GR7 in Andalucia
Walks and Climbs in the Picos de Europa

SWITZERLAND

Alpine Pass Route
Central Switzerland
The Bernese Alps
Tour of the Jungfrau Region
Walking in the Valais
Walking in Ticino
Walks in the Engadine

TECHNIQUES

Geocaching
Indoor Climbing
Lightweight Camping
Map and Compass
Mountain Weather
Moveable Feasts
Rock Climbing
Sport Climbing
The Book of the Bivvy
The Hillwalker's Guide to Mountaineering
The Hillwalker's Manual

MINI GUIDES

Avalanche!
Navigating with a GPS
Navigation
Pocket First Aid and Wilderness Medicine
Snow

For full and up-to-date information on our ever-expanding list of guides, visit our website: **www.cicerone.co.uk**.

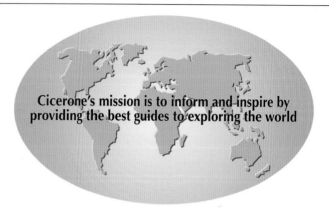

Cicerone's mission is to inform and inspire by providing the best guides to exploring the world

Since its foundation 40 years ago, Cicerone has specialised in publishing guidebooks and has built a reputation for quality and reliability. It now publishes nearly 300 guides to the major destinations for outdoor enthusiasts, including Europe, UK and the rest of the world.

Written by leading and committed specialists, Cicerone guides are recognised as the most authoritative. They are full of information, maps and illustrations so that the user can plan and complete a successful and safe trip or expedition – be it a long face climb, a walk over Lakeland fells, an alpine cycling tour, a Himalayan trek or a ramble in the countryside.

With a thorough introduction to assist planning, clear diagrams, maps and colour photographs to illustrate the terrain and route, and accurate and detailed text, Cicerone guides are designed for ease of use and access to the information.

If the facts on the ground change, or there is any aspect of a guide that you think we can improve, we are always delighted to hear from you.

Cicerone Press
2 Police Square Milnthorpe Cumbria LA7 7PY
Tel: 015395 62069 Fax: 015395 63417
info@cicerone.co.uk www.cicerone.co.uk

CICERONE